FRESH GRADUATES RIGHT START TO SUCCESS AND SIGNIFICANCE

All You Urgently Need to Know to Speed up Your Success, Significance and Satisfaction in Life and Career

Godwill Modibo

Shift Status International (SSI)

Fresh Graduates Right Start To Success And Significance

All You Urgently Need to Know to Speed up Your Success, Significance and Satisfaction in Life and Career

Copyright © 2024 by Godwill Modibo

ISBN: 978-978-773-818-4

Shift Status International (SSI)

Phone: +234 814 447 3652

WhatsApp: +234 802 8278 092

Email: book@shiftstatusinternational.com

freshgraduatescoach@gmail.com

Website: www.shiftstatusinternational.com

Published by: Shift Status Publishing Department of Shift Status International, Lagos, Nigeria.

CONTENTS

ACKNOWLEDGEMENT

I want to acknowledge the Almighty God for the knowledge, understanding, and wisdom of this masterpiece for fresh graduates to right-start their career and life the right way.

I want to acknowledge the support of my wife for her support to make this book work a reality. God reward you, dear.

I want to acknowledge Ozioma Nwakanwa for taking out time to transcript this book work from audio to this book. God bless you!

RECOMMENDATIONS

This course is all-encompassing and has in it every piece of vital information that any fresh graduate who intends to get it right in life and career needs in order to fly. The information contained in this course is so detailed and well spelled out by the tutor, and he deserves his accolades.

Completing the ten modules in this course is one of the best decisions I've ever made in my life. I was enlightened, and I gained a lot of knowledge that will set me on the right track and help me to stand out in my career pursuit and achieve not just success but also satisfaction and significance in life.

So I recommend this course to any recent graduate who is still figuring out what they want to do after school. This course promises to ease you off every doubt and confusion you have about yourself and your career choice and then give you the right push to pursue the career that you are made for- **Ozioma B. N**.

I recently completed the Fresh Graduates Right Start to Success and Significance book, and I must say it is an incredible package that offers all you need to get started in your career and life journey. This ten-topic career and life discovery and development book is thoughtfully and carefully packaged to give you the knowledge, understanding, and wisdom you need to give your career and life a right start.

The book covers several critical topics, including resume writing, CV and cover letter writing, job search, interview skills, negotiation skills, workplace etiquette, and self-development. The course doesn't stop there; it goes on to explore topics such as job transition, work-life balance, self-employment, and Divine

Destiny Work, which are very relevant.

Overall, I highly recommend Fresh Graduates Right Start to Success and Significance to anyone who wants to give their career and life a right start. The book is well-structured, informative, and engaging, and the support proved by the author is invaluable. I have no doubt that anyone who completes this book will be better equipped to achieve success and significance in their career and life journey. - **Ojumu B.**

This is the best book I have ever read about fresh graduates' preparation for work and life. I am very glad I read this book. It's eye-opening! - **Omolola M.**

The author gave several practical initiatives for fresh graduates to grow and create leverage for themselves in different aspects of life. I believe this is a great learning program for every fresh graduate looking to make the next winning step in their career. - **Gideon T. E.**

WHAT YOU WILL LEARN

- Three (3) ways your resume, curriculum vitae (CV), and cover letter (CL) should act on your behalf to your potential employers

- Three (3) things you should not include in your resume, curriculum (CV), and cover letter (CL)

- Three (3) goals your resume, curriculum vitae (CV), and cover letter (CL) should achieve for you

- Three (3) things your job search should be to you as a fresh graduate

- Three (3) ways to reset your mind so that your job search yields results

- Three (3) strategies to employ to get your dream job easily as a fresh graduate

- Three (3) things to do before your interview appointment

- Three (3) things to do during your interview appointment with your potential employer

- Three (3) questions you should not ask your potential employer during your interview appointment as a fresh graduate

- Three (3) negotiation skills to develop and display with your potential employer

- Three (3) mindsets you should not have when negotiating with your potential employer

- Three (3) winning attitudes you should have when negotiating with your potential employer

- Three (3) things to know about your workplace as a fresh graduate

- Three (3) things to always do in your workplace as a fresh graduate

- Three (3) things not to engage in at your workplace as a fresh graduate

- Three (3) reasons why you should self-develop as a fresh graduate

- Three (3) ways to self-develop right and get desired results

- Three (3) seasons of your life where your self-development will profit you the most as a fresh graduate

- Three (3) reasons you should know about work-life balance as a fresh graduate.

- Three (3) benefits of having a work-life balanced lifestyle

- Three (3) areas of your life that you must always keep balanced with your work to stay focused and productive always.

- Three (3) reasons why you may consider job transition as a fresh graduate

- Three (3) things to consider before your job transition as a fresh graduate

- Three (3) ways not to do a job transition as a fresh graduate

- Three (3) reasons why you should consider self-employment as a fresh graduate

- Three (3) benefits of becoming self-employed as a fresh graduate

- Three (3) ways to transit into self-employment as a fresh graduate

- Three (3) things you need to urgently know about your divine destiny Work as a fresh graduate

- Three (3) advantages of practicing your Divine Destiny Work (life purpose profession) as a fresh graduate

- Three (3) disadvantages of not practicing your Divine Destiny Work as a fresh graduate

My intention in writing this book is to give you the right direction that will give you the right start that will enable you to start up and soar like an eagle in your career path and industry in the near future, starting from now.

DEDICATION

This book is dedicated to all fresh graduates all over the world that are starting their career journey with uncertainties and fear of the future. Be assured I got you covered in this book work.

INTRODUCTION

This book is packaged to help fresh graduates not just to attain success but to also achieve satisfaction and significance in life. This book is also packaged to speed up your career life to great success and significance.

As a fresh graduate who desires to succeed in life and in your career, you will agree with me that you need the right starting knowledge to be successful. Therefore, I present to you, **Fresh Graduate, the right start to success and significance** book containing all you urgently need to know to speed up your life and career to success and satisfaction in life.

Therefore, I warmly invite you to come and follow me in this one-in-all book and let me lead you to success and significance in your career because knowledge is power and applied knowledge is powerful.

Who Is This Book For?

Fresh graduates and the unemployed persons who lack the right knowledge on how to right start their career and life from failure and insignificance to success and significance in life.

Requirement For Taking This Book

For this book, as a fresh graduate or unemployed person, be prepared, open-minded, and ready **to unlearn** knowledge that is not working for you, **to relearn** knowledge that could be working for you, and **to learn** lots of new knowledge that would work for you in your career and life pursuit.

Book Description

Fresh Graduates Right Start to Success and Significance is a career and life discovery, development, and delivery book that is thoughtfully and carefully packaged to give your life and career a right start knowledge, understanding, and wisdom you urgently need to right start your life and career and journey to success and significance in life and in your career. Therefore, topics about you and your resume, curriculum vitae, and cover letter were addressed, as well as you and your job search, you and your job interview, you and your negotiation skills, you and your workplace, and you and your self-development that are relevant to your life and career now, and then topics about you and your job transition, you and your work-life balance, you and your self-employment, and you and your Divine Destiny Work that you might need along your career and life pathway were fully covered as well in this book to get you ready now and to prepare you ahead.

Furthermore, Fresh Graduates Right Start to Success and Significance is a ten (10) topic career and life discovery, development, and delivery book with thirty (30) sub-topics, three (3) for each topic. Also, there are ten (10) assignments in this book for you to carry out, one for each topic of this book.

Finally, you who purchased and completed this book will have a thirty (30) day period of opportunity to interact via social media with the author of this book to ask questions as regard life and career matters discussed in this book.

SECTION A: GETTING YOU SMART AS A FRESH GRADUATE

TOPIC 1: YOU AND YOUR RESUME, CURRICULUM VITAE (CV) AND COVER LETTER (CL)

Topic Objective

You will be able to get a better understanding and use of your resume, CV, and cover letter.

Sub-Topic 1:

Three (3) ways your resume, curriculum vitae (CV), and cover letter (CL) should act on your behalf before your potential employer

Having worked with fresh graduates of different higher institutions for over fifteen years, I discovered that many fresh graduates do not know that their resume, CV, and CL should act in these three ways I want to reveal to you in this sub-topic, therefore making many of them unsuccessful in the first stage of recruitment. Let's roll!

1. Your resume, CV, and CL should act as your personal brand ambassador to your potential employer.

As a fresh graduate, I want you to know that you should package your resume, CV, and CL to act as your personal brand ambassador to your potential employer. In achieving this, you should see your resume, CV, and CL as your personal brand ambassador to your potential employer, and therefore be careful of the words and languages you use in your resume, CV, and CL writing. You should not use careless words and slang as you use with your friends when you are with them or family members at home. You should use words and languages that convey to your potential employer the perspectives you want them to have concerning you as the right person for the job.

2. Your resume, CV, and CL should act as your marketing and sales representative to your potential employer.

As a fresh graduate, I want you to know that you should package your resume, CV, and CL to act as your marketing and sales representative to your potential employer. In achieving this, you should see your resume, CV, and CL as your marketing and sales representative to your potential employer, and therefore use words and language in your resume, CV, and CL writing that will convince your potential employer you are the most qualified for the job or that you will be able to add the needed value they seek.

3. Your resume, CV, and CL should act as your interview influencer to your potential employer.

As a fresh graduate, I want you to know that you should package your resume, CV, and CL to act as your interview influencer to your potential employer. In achieving this, you should see your resume, CV, and CL as an interview influencer to your potential employer and therefore use words and language in your resume, CV, and CL writing that will inspire and influence your potential employer's decision to invite you for an interview appointment for the

As a fresh graduate, if you package your resume, CV, and CL with the mindset as I just revealed to you, you will likely be invited for an interview appointment because packaging your resume, CV, and CL with these mindsets has the ability to draw the attention of your potential employer to you and goes further to influence your potential employer to either go your way or go a way that favors you. Yes, it is a sure way of writing a compelling resume, CV, and CL that gets one an interview appointment.

I now encourage you to give it a try now that you have the knowledge that your resume, CV, and CL should act as your personal brand ambassador, marketing and sales representative, and interview influencer on your behalf to your potential employer. Package a resume, CV, and CL to reflect this. I hope you will do just that.

Sub-Topic 2:

Three (3) things you should not include in your resume, curriculum vitae (CV), and cover letter (CL)

Over the years, I found out that many fresh graduates do not know that the resume, CV, and CL they send to their potential employers are most times consciously or unconsciously judged subjectively before they are then judged objectively. This makes it very important as a fresh graduate to know what and what not to include in your resume, CV, and CL you will send to your potential employer, except it is categorically requested you provide such information. Now, let's look at three of these kinds of information you should not include in your resume, CV, and CL as a fresh graduate.

1. You should not include your age and gender in your resume, CV, and CL.

As a fresh graduate, I want you to know that you should not include your age and gender in your resume, CV, and CL you will send to your potential employer unless it is stated as one of the requirements in the job advertisement published. My reason is that even though many organizations might have a policy of equality and no gender bias, some recruiting officers may still not consider your resume, CV, and CL for a certain job position if you are of a certain gender or age bracket. This is true in reality from my experience of over a decade in career-related matters, and you have to keep this knowledge in mind when writing your resume, CV, and CL.

2. You should not include your address in your resume, CV, and CL.

As a fresh graduate, I want you to know that you should not include any of your physical address in your resume, CV, and CL you will send to your potential employer unless it is requested specifically by your potential employer. Including your physical address in your resume, CV, and CL may put you at security risk or other kind of risk if anything goes wrong along the way with you and your recruiter. Remember, you are yet to know your potential employer or recruiter very well, so you must keep certain of your private information secret until you are certain of certain things. Many fresh graduates have become victims by providing such private information, especially from the hands of fake and fraudulent recruiters.

3. You should not include your religion in your resume, CV, and CL.

As a fresh graduate, I want you to know that you should not include your religion in your resume, CV, and CL you send to your potential employer unless it is requested by your potential employer. Religion is a serious and sensitive issue across the globe, and many people, including recruiters, can be at certain times religiously biased toward job seekers. Therefore, as a fresh graduate, it will be unwise to put out such sensitive information about religion in your resume, CV, and CL when it is not requested.

It is certainly unwise to do so.

Remember, my aim in this first section of this book is to get you smart as a fresh graduate. Therefore, take to mind what I reveal to you in this topic and consider it as a guide as you write your resume, CV, and CL, and you will be heading to your interview appointment in no time.

Sub-Topic 3:

Three (3) goals your resume, curriculum vitae (CV), and cover letter (CL) should achieve for you

One of my discoveries over the years as a career coach, counselor, and mentor is that many fresh graduates do not have an idea of what their resume, CV, and CL should achieve for them when they send them to their potential employer. This has made many fresh graduates expect either more or less than what their resume, CV, and CL are meant to achieve for them. Therefore, in this sub-topic, I want to reveal to you three critical goals you should have in mind that your resume, CV, and CL should achieve for you when you send them to your potential employer. This information I am about to pass on to you will help you know what to expect when you send your resume, CV, and CL to your potential employer.

1. Your resume, CV, and CL should get the attention of your potential employer enough to separate you from other applicants.

As a fresh graduate, I want you to know that one of the goals your resume, CV, and CL should achieve for you is to get your potential employer's attention enough to single out your resume, CV, and CL from other resumes, CVs, and CLs and shortlist you for the next stage of the recruitment process. When this is achieved by your resume, CV, and CL and you receive an email, a call, or a text, as the case may be, from your potential employer that you are selected for the next stage of the recruitment process, then your resume, CV, and CL have achieved one of their goals, and you should be proud of yourself and happy about this achievement.

2. Your resume, CV, and CL should get your potential employer to anticipate meeting you for further discussion.

As a fresh graduate, I want you to know that in addition to point one, your resume, CV, and CL should be convincing and compelling enough to stir up the desire of your potential employer wanting to see you to discuss your recruitment further. This is a very important goal that your resume, CV, and CL should achieve for you so that you will be contacted for the next stage of the recruitment process. When your resume, CV, and CL achieve this goal for you, you should congratulate yourself and be proud of yourself as well.

3. Your resume, CV, and CL should get you an interview appointment with your potential employer.

As a fresh graduate, I want you to know that one of the critical goals your resume, CV, and CL should achieve for you is to get you an interview appointment with your potential employer against all odds. This goal is very critical because if your resume, CV, and CL fail to achieve it, you will likely not have the job you seek at that time. Therefore, when your resume, CV, and CL achieve this goal for you, you should know you have done very well with your resume, CV, and CL packaging, and you should jubilate because you have come closer than before to getting the dream job you seek. That is great!

Now, I have an assignment for you to do. This assignment is to get what I have been revealing to you in this topic into you properly so that they can become part of you. Like it is popularly said, practice makes perfect. I do not just want you to be smart in your resume, CV, and CL packaging, but to be perfect as well, and you can achieve this by faithfully carrying out the assignment I give to you at the end of each topic of this book. Haven said that, I encourage you to do this assignment as instructed by me.

Assignment

- Write a resume, curriculum vitae (CV), and cover letter (CL) within the next 7 days, having in mind that your resume, curriculum vitae (CV), and cover letter (CL) should act as your personal brand, sales letter, and ambassador to your potential employer.

TOPIC 2: YOU AND YOUR JOB SEARCH

Topic Objective

You will be able to strategically do your job search and get outstanding results.

Sub-Topic 1

Three (3) things your job search should be to you as a fresh graduate

Over the years, I have seen how many fresh graduates do not apply strategies to their job search and do not give themselves the needed push required to get them a job quickly. This has made many fresh graduates remain jobless for many months or even years after their graduation from school. I therefore desire, through the three sub-topics of this topic, to pass on very important information to you that will inspire and influence you to action so that you can get your dream job in no time from now. Getting your dream job is not as difficult as you think if you will put in the needed efforts I am about to reveal to you. You will discover this soon. Let's go!

1. You should do your job search like you would in paid employment.

As a fresh graduate, I want you to know that if you approach your job search as if you are in paid employment already, you will in a short time get a job placement. In achieving this, I want you to wake up each day with the mindset that your job search is your paid employment, which means you must get ready each day to carry out your daily job descriptions and responsibilities: surfing the internet for new job openings, working on your resume or CV and cover letter, applying for jobs, making calls, sending follow-up emails where necessary, and so on. If you employ the paid employment mindset in your search for a job placement, you will not have any excuse why you should not do what you are supposed to do each day to get yourself out of your unemployment status. True!

2. You should do your job search like you would in self-employment.

As a fresh graduate, I want you to know that another approach you need to apply to your job search is to see it as though you are in self-employment. In achieving this, you will need to have the mindset and attitude of an entrepreneur, which will see you knowing that if you do not take responsibility for your job placement, no one will do so for you. Therefore, you will wake up each morning telling yourself you cannot fail in securing a job, because if you do, you should take responsibility for failing to do what you ought to do. This self-employment mindset for searching for a job placement will make you not to settle for mediocrity daily in your job search but rise up for success by all means.

3. You should do your job search like you would do in a charity employment

As a fresh graduate, I want you to know that, in addition to the points revealed, approaching your job search from a charity employment mindset will get you out of unemployment status faster than you think. In achieving this, you will need to know how employees of charity organizations are expected to act, especially those in the fund-raising department who solicit funds for the cause of their organizations. To achieve their mandates, they go all out to get donors to donate for the cause of their organization. This means you must go all out daily to strategically reach out to people (or organizations) and even to influence your potential employers to consider you for an interview appointment or job placement. Without this mindset, you can watch your unemployment days turn to weeks, weeks turn to months, and months turn to years. You must not allow this to happen to you. Yes, you should not.

Having revealed the three things your job search should be to you, you have no reason to remain unemployed as a fresh graduate. Yes, I believe you can; yes, you can.

Sub-Topic 2:

Three (3) ways to set your mind positively focused so that your job search yields results for you

I have come to understand that many fresh graduates get discouraged and frustrated during their job search and back out from their job search because they do not know how to stay positively focused during the job hunting process. Therefore, in this subtopic, I want to reveal to you three ways you can stay positively focused during your job search so that the result you expect from it becomes a reality for you.

1. Set your mind positively focused by disconnecting from people with negative mindsets and vibes.

As a fresh graduate, I want you to know that if you want your job search to yield results for you as expected, you should consciously and consistently disconnect yourself from people with negative mindsets and vibes during your job search. That is, people who discourage you or want to stop you from searching for a job. In achieving this, you should first believe in your job search and stay positively focused, believing that your search effort will lead you to a job placement one faithful day. This means that you must consciously and consistently set your mind positively focused by disconnecting from people with negative mindsets and vibes who want to make you think and feel that nothing good and positive will comes out of your job search. Yes, you have to!

2. Set your mind positively focused by connecting to people with positive mindsets and vibes.

As a fresh graduate, I want you to know that if you want your job search to yield results for you as expected, you should consciously and consistently connect yourself to people with positive mindsets and vibes during your job search. That is, people who you know will encourage and support you in your job search. In achieving this, you should consciously and consistently determine who and who not to discuss your job search need and effort with so that you will stay positively focused in your job search, hopefully. This means that you must be deliberate to identify and connect with those who will help you stay positively focused so that you can put all your effort into getting a job by all acceptable means in no distance time. This is very important for you to know and do during your job search adventure as a fresh graduate.

3. Set your mind positively focused by reading, listening, and watching inspirational and spiritual stuff.

As a fresh graduate, I want you to know that if you want your job search to yield results for you as expected, you should consciously and consistently commit yourself to reading, listening, and watching inspirational and spiritual materials that will set you positively, powerfully, and hopefully focused during your job search. In achieving this, you should consciously and consistently sort out inspirational and spiritual materials and feed yourself with them during your job search to get your mind and soul positively focused, lifted, and hopeful. You need this because searching for a job can sometimes be draining and stressful, mostly if your job search is taking longer than expected. True!

As a fresh graduate, if you will take into consideration these three counsels I have just given to you in this sub-topic, you will not be discouraged during your job hunting, but you will only stay positively focused, hopeful, and on top of your job search game until you win. You will, in no time, see your job search yield positive results that will cause you to rejoice and make you know that your effort so far is not in vain. True!

Sub-Topic 3:

Three (3) strategies to explore and employ to get your dream job easily

As a career coach, counselor, and mentor to fresh graduates for some good numbers of years now, I have come to realize that many fresh graduates do not consciously employ strategies in their job search for a job placement. Therefore, many of them stay unemployed longer than they should because they were unable to secure the job placement they desired. So, in this subtopic, I will reveal to you three strategies you can explore and employ to get your dream job in no time.

1. Explore and employ past and present relationships and friendships.

As a fresh graduate, I want you to know that you can explore and employ your past and present relationships and friendships in your job search to get a job placement quickly. This means you should be proactive and bold in telling friends and family about your job search. In achieving this, you should be proactive and bold enough to approach your friends and family to discuss your need for a job and ask them how they can help you in your job search or ask them who they know could be of help. You can request from your friends and family to refer or recommend you to a person or organization for a job placement. This job-search strategy will help you eliminate unemployment faster. Give it a try!

2. Explore and employ social gatherings, social networks, and job fairs.

As a fresh graduate, I want you to know that you can explore and employ social gatherings you are invited to, social networks you belong to, and job fairs you attend in your job search to get a job placement quickly. This means that you should be proactive and courageous to identify and reach out to people you meet in social gatherings you are invited to, social networks you belong to, and job fairs you attend to discuss your need for a job placement. In achieving this, you should be proactive and courageous enough to approach people you meet in social gatherings and job fairs you attend and social networks you are involved in to discuss your need for a job placement. I mean, people you have identified can help you get a job placement or refer you for a job placement. Now, know that to be bold and humble to ask for help to secure a job placement is a good and acceptable attitude, so give it a try.

3. Explore and employ social media platforms, websites, and search engines.

As a fresh graduate, I want you to know that you can explore and employ social media platforms, websites, and search engines in your job search to get a job placement quickly. This means that you should be proactive and industrious to go and diligently check out job openings on social media platforms, websites of your potential employers, and search engines to address your need for a job placement. In achieving this, you should be proactive and industrious enough to get yourself busy on social media platforms, websites of your potential employers you know of, and search engines using key words in your search.

As a fresh graduate, I want you to know that often times, it is the proactive, bold, courageous, industrious, and smart job seekers that get themselves out of their unemployment status faster, and you need to be one of them now to get yourself a job placement sooner than expected. Now, I have an assignment for you.

Assignment

- Discuss your need for a job boldly with at least five (5) friends and family for the next 7 days.

- Attend at least three (3) social gatherings you are invited to and discuss your need for a job boldly with at least five people you meet in each of them.

TOPIC 3: YOU AND YOUR JOB INTERVIEW

Topic Objective

You will be able to inspire and influence your potential employer to get your dream job.

Sub-Topic 1:

Three (3) Things to Do Before Your Interview Appointment

My experience with many fresh graduates revealed to me that many of them do not know what to do before their interview appointment. This is the reason many fresh graduates fail to impress their potential employer during their job interview appointment and then fail to secure the job they desire. Therefore, in this subtopic, I will reveal to you three things you should do before your interview appointment. These are three things you should do before your interview appointment that will give you an advantage during your job interview as a fresh graduate. Let's roll!

1. Do Research On Your Potential Employer.

As a fresh graduate, I want you to know that you should do thorough and proper research about your potential employer before you go for your job interview appointment. In achieving this, you should get every possible information you can concerning your potential employer. That is, getting information about what and what your potential employer stands for and does as an organization. Getting such critical information about your potential employer before your job interview appointment will position you ahead of other applicants and also make you sound intelligent and smart before your potential employer during your job interview appointment. Furthermore, to note is that using information you researched out about your potential employer during your interview appointment will make you look like you are already a part of the organization before your potential employer. True!

2. Do Research On Your Potential Employer's Competitors And Understand What Differentiates Them.

As a fresh graduate, I want you to know that you should do investigative research about your potential employer's competitors to know what and what differentiates your potential employer's organization from them. In achieving this, you should get to work seeking to know your potential employer's competitors by carrying out investigative research on them and comparing them to your potential employer's organization to know what makes them different from your potential employer's organization. If you do this, you will be armed with critical information that will show your potential employer during your job interview appointment that you are truly prepared and ready to add value, and you will likely get the job position you seek. True!

3. Do Prepare To Present How You Will Add Value To Your Potential Employer Based On What You Have Discovered From Your Research.

As a fresh graduate, I want you to know that you should smartly prepare to add value to your potential employer based on the information you have gathered from your research. In achieving this, you should take out time to carefully go through the information you have gotten from your research and make them your own with a readiness to smartly and confidently present them to your potential employer in line with the questions asked you. If you prepare this way and present your answers to your potential employer's questions from a point of relevant and sound knowledge based on your research, you will be amazed at how impressed your potential employer can be and how pleased they will be to have you hired immediately.

Sub-Topic 2:

Three (3) Things to Do During Your Interview Appointment with Your Potential Employer

Having come a long way with coaching, counseling, and mentoring of fresh graduates, I can categorically say that many fresh graduates do not know what to do during their job interview appointment with their potential employer, and this has made many fresh graduates fail in their job interview with their potential employer. Therefore, in this subtopic, I will reveal to you three things you should do during your job interview appointment with your potential employer.

1. Be a Good and Attentive Listener by Not Interrupting When Your Potential Employer Speaks.

As a fresh graduate, I want you to know that the foremost thing you should do during your job interview with your potential employer is to be a good and attentive listener to them when they are asking you questions or speaking to you. In order to achieve this, you should learn and prepare before your interview appointment how to be a good and attentive listener when someone is speaking to you. This means that you must learn beforehand not to interrupt when people speak to you, because if you do, you will likely do the same with your potential employer during your job interview. If you do not interrupt your potential employer during your job interview, you will impress your potential employer with such quality and make your potential employer, in addition to other things, want to consider hiring you. Remember, first impression matters!

2. Be a Good Communicator by Keeping Your Voice Volume Cordial With Good Body Language.

As a fresh graduate, I want you to know that the second thing you should learn and prepare to do before your job interview appointment is that you should be a good communicator who speaks with a voice volume that is cordial and do not show arrogance or overconfidence before your potential employer. In achieving this, you should practice how to speak with your friends and family with a voice volume that is cordial with good body language before your job interview appointment with your potential employer. This is very important for you to achieve because no matter what you are saying to your potential employer during your job interview appointment, if your potential employer perceives you as being arrogant and proud in the way and manner you speak, your hiring chance could be slim.

3. Be Confident and Relaxed As You Give Answers to the Questions Asked Of You.

As a fresh graduate, I want you to know that one thing you should do during your job interview appointment with your potential employer is to be confident and relaxed to give answers to the questions being asked of you. This requires learning and practicing not to be afraid or anxious around authorities or people you respect. Anxiety before your potential employer will send a wrong signal to your potential employer that you are not prepared and mature enough to fit into the job role you seek. Therefore, you must learn before your job interview appointment how to be confident and relaxed to speak, and this will pay off when you finally show up to be with your potential employer on your job interview appointment day.

Sub-Topic 3:

Three (3) Questions You Should Not Ask Your Potential Employer during Your Job Interview Appointment as a Fresh Graduate

Having seen and heard several times the questions fresh graduates ask their potential employers during their job interview, which disqualified them before their potential employer, I intend in this sub-topic to reveal to you three questions you should not ask your potential employer during your job interview appointment. Asking your potential employer these three questions I am about to reveal to you during your job interview will put you in a bad light before your potential employer.

1. Do Not Ask If They Pay Over Time.

As a fresh graduate, I want you to know that you should not ask your potential employer during your job interview appointment if your potential employer pays over time. In achieving this, you should be conscious not to ask such questions when your potential employer asks if you have any questions to ask during your job interview. This is very important because asking such a question as a fresh graduate will show your potential employer your unwillingness to give your all and best to the job role you seek, and I know such encounters and experiences are not what you want to have with your potential employer during your job interview. True!

2. Do Not Ask If They Observe Public Holidays And Weekend Breaks.

As a fresh graduate, I want you to know that you should not ask your potential employer during your job interview if your potential employer observes public holidays and weekend breaks.

In achieving this, you should be conscious not to ask such questions when your potential employer asks if you have any questions to ask during your job interview. This is very important because asking such a question as a fresh graduate will prove to your potential employer your lack of interest in working in the job position you seek with your potential employer. And I know this is not the kind of negative impression you will want your potential employer to have towards you during and after your job interview appointment with your potential employer. True!

3. Do Not Ask If They Give Annual Or Sick Leave.

As a fresh graduate, I want you to know that you should not ask your potential employer during your job interview appointment if your potential employer gives annual or sick leave. In achieving this, you should be conscious not to ask such questions when your potential employer asks if you have any questions to ask during your job interview. This is very important because asking such a question as a fresh graduate will show your potential employer your lack of commitment already. And I know this is not what you want your potential employer to perceive about you during your job interview appointment. True!

At this point, I will advise you to ask your potential employer, as a fresh graduate, just this question: ask if there are growth and development opportunities when working with them. This will show your potential employer your interest in the job role you seek and your willingness to stay in the position for a long time while giving your best. Now, I have an assignment for you to do. This assignment will help get my message on this topic to you. Therefore, carry them out.

Assignment

- **List at least 10 values you can add to your potential**

employer's organization and recite them to yourself daily.

- Practice being a good listener and communicator with friends and family in the next 21 days.

TOPIC 4: YOU AND YOUR NEGOTIATION SKILLS

Topic Objective

You will be able to negotiate with your potential employer to their advantage

Sub-Topic 1:

Three (3) Negotiation Skills to Develop and Display with Your Potential Employer

One very interesting thing I have discovered over the years working with fresh graduates is that many Fresh graduates do not for once think that negotiation is involved during their job interview appointment with their potential employer. Many Fresh Graduates are ignorant that they are actually negotiating with their potential employer during their job interview appointment when they and their potential employer are discussing various terms and conditions of the job position they seek. Therefore, I want to through these three lessons bring to your awareness that you are actually negotiating during your job interview with your potential employer and to inform you how to go about it to get the best out of your negotiation with your potential employer. Let's go!

1. Develop And Display The Skill To Demand What You Want Diplomatically

As a fresh graduate, I want you to know that you will be actually negotiating with your potential employer during your job interview when both of you are discussing terms and conditions of your job position during and after your job interview appointment. Therefore, you need to start developing and displaying the negotiating skill of demanding what you want diplomatically. In achieving this, you must now deliberately start learning how to demand what you want diplomatically and not arrogantly from your friends and family. This is very important because if you fail to learn how to ask for what you want diplomatically, you may end getting a negative response from your potential employer and I know this is not what you want to see happen for you with your potential employer from the start of your working relationship.

2. Develop and Display the Skill to Give Alternative Options Nicely When and Where Necessary

As a fresh graduate, I want you to know that you will be actually negotiating with your potential employer during your job interview when both of you are discussing terms and conditions of your job position during and after your job interview appointment. Therefore, you need to start developing and displaying the negotiating skill of suggesting alternative options nicely. In achieving this, you must begin to learn how to intelligently generate and present alternative options nicely to those you know or those you transact one or two things with, so that you can do the same to your potential employer during your job interview appointment when what your potential employer is being offer you is less or not accordance to what you expect from your potential employer. This is very important for you to learn to do because that might just be your saving grace to have what you desire from your potential employer. True!

3. Develop And Display The Skill To Compromise Smartly

When And Where Necessary

As a fresh graduate, I want you to know that you will be actually negotiating with your potential employer during your job interview appointment when both of you are discussing terms and conditions of your job position during and after your job interview appointment. Therefore, you need to develop and display the negotiating skill of compromising smartly when and where necessary. In achieving this, you must begin to learn the negotiating skill of compromising smartly when and where necessary by letting some things be when you bargain with your friends and family or with people you interact with in other areas of your life. Good to know at this point is that compromising is not always negative as many think, especially when it is done smartly. You can compromise smartly as a good negotiation skill when and where necessary when negotiating with your potential employer during your job interview appointment or after as the case may be.

Sub-Topic 2:

Three (3) Mindsets You Should Not Have When Negotiating With Your Potential Employer

Carrying a wrong mindset into a negotiation with a potential employer during a job interview has caused many fresh graduates disadvantage with their potential employer because as I have discovered over the years, many fresh graduates are ignorant of the kind of mindsets they should have when going for their job interview with their potential employer. Therefore, I want to reveal to you three mindsets you should not have when negotiating with your potential employer during your job interview appointment.

1. Do Not Have "I Must Have My Way" Mindset

As a fresh graduate, I want you to know you should not carry to your job interview appointment with your potential employer an "I must have my way" mindset. This is because this mindset can put you in a bad light before your potential employer and therefore, have the ability to make you lose your chance of being hired by your potential employer. In achieving this, you must consciously know and avoid going to your job interview appointment with your potential employer with the mindset of "I must have my way", especially when you and your potential employer are discussing the terms and conditions of the job position you seek. Having a mindset of "I must have my way" or "I must have what I want" shows you are not considerate whether your potential employer is able to afford what you are proposing or not. All you care about is yourself and yourself alone. That is a selfish mindset and it is not good to carry such mindset with you to your job interview with your potential employer. True!

2. Do Not Have "Win And Loose" Mindset

As a fresh graduate, I want you to know you should not carry to your job interview with your potential employer a "win and lose" mindset. This is because this mindset can put you in a bad light before your potential employer and therefore have the ability to make you lose your chance of being hired by your potential employer. In achieving this, you must consciously know and avoid going to your job interview appointment with your potential employer with the mindset of "win and lose" especially when you and your potential employer are discussing the terms and conditions of the job position you seek. Having a "win and lose" mindset means you having a mindset that you do not mind if your potential employer have value for what they got from the negotiation or not, all you know is that you got what you want. This is not a good mindset to have during your job interview with your potential employer. True!

3. Do Not Have "If I Walk Away, They Are Finished" Mindset

As a fresh graduate, I want you to know you should not carry to your job interview appointment with your potential employer an "if I walk away, they are finished" mindset. This is because this mindset can put you in a bad light before your potential employer and therefore have the ability to make you lose your chance of being hired by your potential employer. In achieving this, you must consciously know and avoid going to your job interview appointment with your potential employer with the mindset of "if I walk away, they are finished" especially when you and your potential employer are discussing the terms and conditions of the job position you seek. Having an "if I walk away, they are finished" mindset means you having a mindset that make you think that since you being considered the best candidate to be hired for the job position you seek, at this point without you, your potential employer cannot do without you if you decide to walk away and most times, your body language reveals this to your potential employer. This is not a good mindset to have during your job interview appointment with your potential employer. True!

Sub-Topic 3:

Three (3) Winning Attitudes You Should Have When Negotiating With Your Potential Employer

Having found out over the years that many fresh graduates do not know what attitudes they should have when going for their job interview appointment with their potential employer, I want to in this sub-topic reveal to you three winning attitudes you should have when you go to your job interview appointment with your potential employer. This revelation becomes necessary because being a fresh graduates who is unaware of what kind of attitude you should have when you go to your job interview appointment with your potential employer or when you are negotiating with your potential employer during your job interview appointment can cost you a great price of not being hired by your potential employer and that could be saddening.

1. Have The Winning Attitude Of Connecting Your Demands To Values You Want To Add

As a fresh graduate, I want you to know that you should have a winning attitude of connecting your demands to the values you want to add to your potential employer than just demanding without connecting to a corresponding value you want add to your potential employer. This is very important that you consciously know and do during your job interview negotiation with your potential employer. In achieving this, you must be conscious of your demand to your potential employer during your job interview appointment negotiation by making sure you add value to your demand. If you do, your potential employer will be more dispose to grant you your request compared to when you do not pointing to the value you will add to your potential employer. True!

2. Have The Winning Attitude Of Showing Consideration

As a fresh graduate, I want you to know that you should have a winning attitude of showing consideration to your potential employer than just demanding without considering what effect your demand will have on your potential employer. This is very important that you consciously know and have during your job interview negotiation with your potential employer. In achieving this, you must be conscious of your demand to your potential employer during your job interview appointment negotiation by making sure you always consider what impact your demand will have on your potential employer. If you do, your potential employer will notice your kindness and be more dispose to grant you your request. True!

3. Have The Winning Attitude Of Win And Win

As a fresh graduate, I wants you to know that you should have a winning attitude of win and win towards your potential employer during your job interview appointment with your potential employer than just wanting to have wins over your potential employer without you also checking whether your potential employer is having wins as well. This is very important that you consciously know and have during your job interview negotiation with your potential employer. In achieving this, you must be conscious of your demand to your potential employer during your job interview negotiation by making sure that you and your potential employer gain from your demands and both of you are satisfy and happy with the outcome of the negotiation. If you do, your potential employer will notice your uncommon attitude and be more dispose to grant you your request. True!

At this junction, I have an assignment for you to get what I have be revealing to you in this topic to get into you. Take time to do this assignment and you will be better for it.

Assignment

- Consciously and consistently learn to make demands diplomatically from friends and family in the next 21 days

- Consciously and consistently take a compromising smart position in the discussions you will be having with friends and family in the next 21 days

- Consciously and consistently take a win and win position in the interactions you will be having with friends and family in the next 21 days.

TOPIC 5: YOU AND YOUR WORKPLACE

Topic Objective:

You will be able to know how to manage yourself around your workplace to their advantage.

Sub-Topic 1:

Three (3) Things to Know About Your Workplace As A Fresh Graduate

Many fresh graduates do not initially have the right knowledge of what a workplace is and, as a result, have led themselves into unpleasant situations in their first few months or years in their workplace, and this has also made many fresh graduates victims of dubious colleagues who take advantage of their ignorance to set them up for failure in their workplace. This is my sad discovery. Therefore, in this sub-topic, I am going to reveal to you three things you should know about what your workplace is, so that you will be safe and sure knowing that you are doing the right thing in your workplace. Let's roll!

1. Know That Your Workplace Is A Place Of Assigned Responsibilities.

As a fresh graduate, I want you to know that your workplace is a place of assigned responsibilities where you are expected to carry out sets of outlined duties and tasks assigned to the job position you are hired for. Therefore, you are not expected to do everything you see your other colleagues do in your workplace. In achieving this, you must consciously know and begin to prepare and program your mind to accept that you are hired for a specific job role that has a specific set of assigned responsibilities or duties that you are expected to perform or carry out each day, each week, each month, and each year in or out of your workplace. Understanding this as a fresh graduate will not make you a victim in your workplace by responding to calls by other colleagues to assist them in fulfilling their own task or meeting their own target when you have not fulfilled your own task or met your own target for the day, week, month, or year that you are officially employed to do.

2. Know That Your Workplace Is A Place Of Respect.

As a fresh graduate, I want you to know that your workplace is a place of respect where you are expected to give respect to your colleagues, but more especially to colleagues who are in official positions, duties, and authorities higher than your own in your workplace. Therefore, you are not to see and treat each and every one of your colleagues as though they are all at your official job position level. If you do, you may pay dearly for it. In achieving this, you are expected to consciously know and begin to prepare and program your mind to accept that you and every other of your colleagues in your workplace are not at the same official job position level as you, and you must not see and treat every one of your colleagues the same way as you do with your friends. This is very true to know and to keep to.

3. Know That Your Workplace Is A Place Of Appreciating Relationships.

As a fresh graduate, I want you to know that your workplace is a place of appreciating relationships where you are expected to work with other of your colleagues in partnership as a team to meet either daily, weekly, monthly, or yearly targets and achieve departmental and organizational goals and vision. Therefore, you are not expected to have an independent working mindset or attitude in your workplace when you are expected to relate with your other colleagues to see that the work for the day, week, month, or year as planned, projected, and budgeted for is achieved. In achieving this, you must consciously recognize and begin to prepare and program your mind to appreciate both personal and official relationships in your workplace that help meet departmental and organizational goals. You must not treat this point lightly because employers will waste no time to relieve an employee who is found not to appreciate personal and official relationships that are meant to assist in meeting departmental and organization targets, goals, and vision. Take this to heart seriously as a fresh graduate.

Sub-Topic 2:

Three (3) Things To Always Do In Your Workplace As A Fresh Graduate

Being ignorant of what to do in your workplace as a fresh graduate has made many fresh graduates pay dearly in their first few months or years in their workplace, and this is a great concern to me because of my passion for fresh graduates. Therefore, in this subtopic, I will reveal to you three things you should always do in your workplace as a fresh graduate. If you take these three things to heart as a fresh graduate at your workplace and diligently do them, you will stand out from other new intakes there. True!

1. Always Do Your Duties And Meet Your Targets, Both Officially And Unofficially Assigned To You.

As a fresh graduate, I want you to know that you should always do your duties and meet your targets as they are officially and unofficially assigned to you. This is very important that you know and do wholeheartedly because you are not expected for any reason to complain or be negligent to official and unofficial duties and targets assigned to you in your workplace. In achieving this, you should consciously know and start getting yourself ready to do whatsoever you are assigned to do in your workplace that is aimed at meeting the expectations of your department or your organization. This is very important to know and note, and more importantly, to do in your workplace.

2. Always Abide By The Rules And Regulations Guiding Employees Within Your Workplace And Organization.

As a fresh graduate, I want you to know that you should always abide by the rules and regulations guiding employees within your workplace and organization. This is very important that you know and do wholeheartedly because you are not expected for any reason or reasons to rebel, disobey, and break the rules and regulations guiding employees within your workplace and organization that keep your workplace and organization in sanity for all to work peacefully and productively. In achieving this, you should consciously know and start getting yourself ready to abide by and obey each and every rule and regulation guiding employees within your workplace and organization without complaints. This is very important to know and note, and more importantly, to do in your workplace.

3. Always Keep To The Departmental And Organizational Culture Of Your Workplace.

As a fresh graduate, I want you to know that you should always keep to the departmental and organizational culture of your workplace. This is very important that you know and do wholeheartedly because you are not expected for any reason to think, speak, and act contrary to the departmental and organizational culture of your workplace that makes working together to meet departmental and organizational goals and vision possible. In achieving this, you should consciously know and start getting yourself ready to keep to departmental and organizational culture in your workplace without complaints. This is very important to know and note as well, and more importantly, to do in your workplace.

Sub-Topic 3:

Three (3) Things Not To Engage In At Your Workplace as a Fresh Graduate

Engaging in certain things because of ignorance has put many fresh graduates in the bad light before their colleagues and bosses and, in the long run, sabotage their working relationships and opportunities within their workplace. This is sad! Therefore, in this sub-topic, I will reveal to you three things you should not do or engage in your workplace. If you take these three things to heart as a fresh graduate new at your workplace, you will be better and glad you did. True!

1. Do Not Engage In Workplace Parading.

As a fresh graduate, I want you to know you should not engage in workplace parading. This means that you should not engage yourself in moving around offices and premises in your workplace for non-official duties and assignments. This is because this practice will soon put you in bad light with your colleagues as well as your bosses, as the case may be. In achieving this, you should consciously know and get yourself disciplined not to engage in workplace parading by moving about offices and premises of your workplace when it is not necessary. If you do as a fresh graduate who is new in your workplace, your colleagues as well as your bosses will notice your attitude and have some respect for you, and you will be watched for something good coming. True!

2. Do Not Engage In Workplace Politics.

As a fresh graduate, I want you to know you should not engage in workplace politics. This means that you should not engage yourself in joining colleagues to pull down other colleagues or bosses in your workplace. This is because this practice will soon put you in bad light with your colleagues as well as your bosses, as the case may be. In achieving this, you should consciously know and get yourself disciplined not to engage in workplace politics by joining colleagues to pull down other colleagues or bosses in your workplace when it is not necessary. If you do as a fresh graduate who is new in your workplace, your colleagues as well as your bosses will notice your attitude and have some respect for you, and you will be watched for something good coming. True!

3. Do Not Engage In Workplace Poking.

As a fresh graduate, I want you to know you should not engage in workplace poking. This means that you should not engage yourself in getting into matters that do not concern you, or your opinion was not asked in your workplace. This is because this practice will soon put you in bad light with your colleagues as well as your bosses, as the case may be. In achieving this, you should consciously know and get yourself disciplined not to engage in workplace poking by not getting yourself into matters that do not concern you or your opinion was not asked in your workplace when it is not necessary. If you do as a fresh graduate who is new in your workplace, your colleagues as well as your bosses will notice your attitude and have some respect for you, and you will be watched over time for something good coming. True!

Now, I have an assignment for you to get what I have revealed to you in this topic into you properly. Take out time to carefully carry out this assignment, and you will not regret it.

Assignment

- **Research your potential employer's website and social media platforms for the next three days to get tips on some of their rules, regulations, and cultures and start practicing them as they fit into your circumstances.**

TOPIC 6: YOU & YOUR SELF DEVELOPMENT

Topic Objective:

You will be able to see the need to self-develop for your advancement.

Sub-Topic 1:

Three (3) Reasons Why You Should Self-Develop As A Fresh Graduate

As a career coach, counselor, and mentor to so many fresh graduates of different higher institutions, I have come to realize that many fresh graduates do not know that they should self-develop or self-educate themselves apart from their conventional education that they have just gone through. I also discovered that even those who know about self-development do not know what to self-develop themselves on, and even sadly, many do not know how to go about their self-development rightly to profit them. This has made many fresh graduates remain stagnated or irrelevant in their chosen career and, for many others, in life as well. This is the reason why, in this sub-topic, I will be revealing to you three reasons you should self-develop or self-improve as a fresh graduate. Let's go!

1. You Should Self-Develop To Be Alert In Your Career And In Life.

As a fresh graduate, I want you to know that you should self-develop deliberately so that you will be alert in your career and in life. What do I mean by this? In other words, you should self-improve to stay current in your career and life. This is very important for you to know and to consciously and consistently stay informed in your career and in life. In achieving this, you should consciously and consistently set out time each day, each week, each month, and each year to self-develop by deliberately going all out to search and get informative materials and ways in the area of your career and in each area of your life to stay alert or informed in your career and in life as well. This cannot be overemphasized because the benefits and profits of self-developing far outweigh the investment of your time and resources you will put into it. Therefore, if you consciously and regularly self-develop or self-improve in the area of your career and each area of your life, you will one day become one of the sort after persons in your career and in life, even outside your career. And this is a wonderful achievement to look forward to in your career and in life as a fresh graduate. True!

2. You Should Self-Develop To Be Alive In Your Career And Life

As a fresh graduate, I want you to know that you should self-develop deliberately so that you will be alive in your career and in life. What do I mean by this? Self-develop or "improve to stay relevant in your career and life. This is very important for you to know and to consciously and consistently do to stay relevant in your career and in life. In achieving this, you should consciously and consistently set out time each day, each week, each month, and each year to self-develop yourself by deliberately going all out to search and get relevant materials and ways in the area of your career and in each area of your life to stay relevant in your career and in life as well. This cannot be overemphasized, as I have once said, because the benefits and profits of self-developing in your career and in life far outweigh the investment of your time and resources you will put into it. Therefore, if you consciously and regularly self-develop or self-improve yourself in the area of your career and in each area of your life, you will one day, as I have said earlier, become one of the sort of people in your career and in life, and even outside your career. And this is a wonderful achievement to look forward to in your career and in life as a fresh graduate. True!

3. You Should Self-Develop To Stay Ahead In Your Career And Life.

As a fresh graduate, I want you to know that you should self-develop deliberately so that you will be ahead in your career and in life. What do I mean by this? I mean that you should self-develop or self-improve to be above and beyond what is going on in your career and in life. This is important for you to know and to consciously and consistently do to stay ahead in your career and in life. In achieving this, you should consciously and consistently set out time each day, each week, each month, and each year to self-develop by deliberately going all out to search and get cutting-edge materials and ways in the area of your career and in each area of your life to stay ahead in your career and in life as well. This cannot be overemphasized because the benefits and profits of self-developing to stay ahead far outweigh the investment of your time and resources that you will put into it. Therefore, if you consciously and regularly self-develop or self-improve in the area of your career and in each area of your life, you will one day, as I have said earlier and I will say again here, become one of the sort of people in your career and in life, and even outside your career. And this is an outstanding achievement to look forward to in your career and in life as a fresh graduate. True!

Sub-Topic 2:

Three (3) Ways to Self-Develop Right and Get Desired Results as

A Fresh Graduate

To self-develop right is very important because self-developing wrongly will not only lead to getting undesired results from your self-development, it can be very disadvantageous as well. This is very true. I discovered that while some fresh graduates desire to self-develop themselves, they are ignorant of how to go about it or what to self-develop. Therefore, in this sub-topic, I will be revealing to you three ways you can self-develop yourself right to get desired results. So I want you to pay close attention to what I will be informing you about in this lesson.

1. Self-Develop Your Career In A Way That Aligns With Your Purpose.

As a fresh graduate, I want you to know that you should self-develop in the way of your career to align with your life purpose. What do I mean by this? I mean, you should deliberately self-develop in such a way that your career has a connecting link with your life purpose that you have discovered and are willing to see fulfilled. This is very important to know and to consciously and consistently seek to achieve through your self-development because your success in your career and satisfaction in life depend on it to a very reasonable extent. In achieving this, you should consciously discover your purpose in life and consistently seek out relevant materials and ways to link and align your career to this life purpose that you have discovered. Truth be told, this is the winning advantage and cutting-edge of many experts of various career paths that makes them look extraordinary and keeps them looking outstanding in the eyes of other people in their various areas of career interest. Therefore, if you will deliberately do as I am currently informing and instructing you as a fresh graduate, the sky will not only be your limit; your limit will be above and beyond the sky. True!

2. Self-Develop Your Career In A Way That Aligns With Your Potential.

As a fresh graduate, I want you to know that you should self-develop in the way of your career to align with your potential. What do I mean by this? I mean, you should deliberately self-develop in such a way that your career has a connecting link with your potentials (talents and gifts) that you have discovered and are willing to use to fulfill your career and purpose in life. This is very important to know and to consciously and consistently seek to achieve through your self-development because your survival in your career and success in life depend on it to a very reasonable extent. In achieving this, you should consciously discover your potentials in life and consistently seek out relevant materials and ways to link and align your career to these potentials that you have discovered. Truth be told once more, this is the winning approach and cutting-edge of many experts in various career paths that makes them look extraordinary and keeps them looking outstanding in the eyes of other people in their various areas of career interest. Therefore, if you will deliberately do as I am currently informing and instructing you as a fresh graduate, the sky will not only be your limit; your limit will be above and beyond the sky. True!

3. Self-Develop In The Way Of Your Career To Align With Your Personality.

As a fresh graduate, I want you to know that you should self-develop in the way of your career to align with your personality. What do I mean by this? I mean, you should deliberately self-develop in such a way that your career has a connecting link with your personality that you have discovered and are willing to use to express and manifest your career and purpose in life. This is very important for you to know and to consciously and consistently seek to achieve through your self-development because your charisma in your career and carriage in life depends on it to a very reasonable extent. In achieving this, you should consciously discover your personality in life and consistently seek out relevant materials and ways to link and align your career to this personality that you have discovered. Truth be told, once again, this is the winning secret and cutting-edge of many experts of various career paths that makes them look extraordinary and keeps them looking outstanding in the eyes of other people in their various areas of career interest. Therefore, if you will deliberately do as I am currently informing and instructing you as a fresh graduate, the sky will not only be your limit; as I have said consistently in this module, your limit will be above and beyond the sky. True!

Sub-Topic 3:

Three (3) Seasons of Your Life Where Your Self-Development Will Profit You The Most As A Fresh Graduate

I discovered over the years in my working relationships with fresh graduates that many fresh graduates do not want to consider self-development because many of them do not see reasons to do so. Therefore, to take away this from many fresh graduates as possible, I have considered including this topic in this topic and further including this sub-topic in this topic. So in this sub-topic, I will be revealing to you three reasons why you, as a fresh graduate, should urgently and deliberately consider and engage in self-development early enough in your career and in life. So let's roll!

1. In The Season Of Your Career Advancement And Work-Life Balance Decision-Making

As a fresh graduate, I want you to know that you should urgently and deliberately consider and engage in self-development or self-improvement. This is because in no distant time in your career path and life journey you may be needing the results from your self-development in making informed decisions as regards your career advancement and work-life balance desires. True! Therefore, you should consciously consider self-development and consistently self-develop so that when you need to make this very important and critical decision of your career and life as it relates to your career advancement and work-life balance desire, you will not be found wanting by taking uninformed decisions that could cost you pain and regret in your career and life in the long run. In achieving this, you should now urgently see the need to self-develop or self-improve yourself and faithfully commit to self-development until you will be needing its results in your life to make informed decisions that will favor your career advancement and work-life balance decisions and keep you on top of the game of your career and life. Will you?

2. In The Season Of Your Job Transition, Decision-Making

As a fresh graduate, I want you to know that you should urgently and deliberately consider and engage in self-development or self-improvement. This is because in no distant time in your career path and life journey you may be needing the results from your self-development in your life in making informed decisions as regards your job transition desire. True! Therefore, you should consciously consider self-development and consistently self-develop yourself so that when you need to make this very important and critical decision of your career and life as it relates to your job transition desire, you will not be found wanting to take uninformed decisions that could cost you pain and regret in your career and life in the long run. In achieving this, you should now urgently see the need to self-develop or self-improve and faithfully commit to self-development until you will be needing its results in your life to make informed decisions that will favor your job transition decision and keep you on top of the game of your career and life. Will you?

3. In The Season Of Your Self-Employment Decision-Making

As a fresh graduate, I want you to know that you should urgently and deliberately consider and engage in self-development or self-improvement. This is because in no distant time in your career path and life journey you may be needing the results from your self-development in your life in making informed decisions as regards your self-employment desire. True! Therefore, you should consciously consider self-development and consistently self-develop yourself so that when you need to make this very important and critical decision of your career and life as it relates to your self-employment desire, you will not be found wanting to take an uninformed decision that will cost you sorrow and regret in your career and life in the long run. In achieving this, you should now urgently see the need to self-develop or self-improve and faithfully commit to self-development until you will be needing its results in your life to make informed decisions that will favor your self-employment decision and keep you on top of the game of your career and life. Will you?

Now, I have an assignment for you to do. Do it as I have instructed you and enjoy the benefit for a lifetime.

Assignment

- **What do you think is your purpose in life and your personality? Write them down.**

- **List one to three potentials you believe that you have and list three things you can do in the next 7 days to self-develop them and get into action.**

TOPIC 7: YOU & YOUR WORK-LIFE BALANCE

Topic Objective

You will be able to know what work-life balance is and when to balance your work and life.

Sub-Topic 1

Three (3) Reasons Why You Should Know About Work-Life Balance As A Fresh Graduate

Understanding that many fresh graduates do not have an idea of what work-life balance is inspired me to include this topic in this book. This is because it is very important from the beginning of your career that you know what work-life is because your ignorance of it can cause you great loss and pain in your career path in the near future. Many employees, for the love of their careers, have overworked themselves to regret and, for some, to death. This must not be your case. Therefore, in this subtopic, I will reveal to you three reasons you should know about work-life balance from the start of your career journey. Let's roll!

1. You Should Know About Work-Life Balance Because It Will Determine The Level Of Joy And Peace You Will Have In Your Life And In Your Career.

As a fresh graduate, I want you to know that it is good and great to know about work-life balance from the start of your career journey outside school because work-life balance will determine the level of joy and peace you will have in your life and career in the long run in your career journey. True! This is because if your work and life are out of balance, some areas of your life and career, or in some cases, your entire life and career, can plunge into serious emotional crises and chaos, and I know this is not what you want to see happen to you in the near future along your career path. Therefore, in achieving a work-life balance where your work and life are in order as you desire, plan, and want to see it be, you should know about work-life balance now and then wholeheartedly commit to it as you consciously and consistently self-develop to achieve it from the start of your career and as you journey along your career path to success and satisfaction. If you do, you will encounter and experience an uncommon level of fulfillment and peace in your life and career that attracts the attention of your colleagues who are ignorant of a work-life balance lifestyle to ask you how you do it, and I know you will be nice enough to show them your secret.

2. You Should Know About Work-Life Balance Because It Will Determine Your Level Of Mental Healthiness And Productivity In Life And In Your Career.

As a fresh graduate, I want you to know that it is wise and smart to know about work-life balance from the start of your career journey outside school because work-life balance will determine the level of mental healthiness and productivity you will have in your life and career and in the long run in your career journey. True! This is because if your work and life are out of balance, some areas of your life and career, or in some cases, your entire life and career, can plunge into serious health crises and chaos. And I know this is not what you want to see happen to you in the near future along your career path. Therefore, in achieving a work-life balance where your work and life are in order as you desire, plan, and want to see it be, you should know about work-life balance now and then wholeheartedly commit to it as you consciously and consistently self-develop to achieve it from the start of your career and as you journey along your career path to success and satisfaction. If you do, you will encounter and experience an uncommon level of mental healthiness and productivity in your life and career that attracts the attention of your colleagues who are ignorant of a work-life balance lifestyle to ask you how you do it, and I know you will be nice enough to show them the way.

3. You Should Know About Work-Life Balance Because It Will Determine How Long You Will Live In Life Or How Far You Will Go In Your Career.

As a fresh graduate, I want you to know that it is wise and smart to know about work-life balance from the start of your career journey outside school because work-life balance will determine how long you will live in life or how far you will go in your career in the long run. True! This is because if your work and life are out of balance, some areas of your life and career, or in some cases, your entire life and career, can plunge into serious life-and-death crises and chaos. And I know this is not what you want to see happen to you in the near future along your career path. Therefore, in achieving a work-life balance where your work and life are in order as you desire, plan, and want to see it be, you should know about work-life balance now and then wholeheartedly commit to it as you consciously and consistently self-develop to achieve it from the start of your career and as you journey along your career path to success and satisfaction. If you do, you will encounter and experience an expected long life in your life and career that attracts the attention of your colleagues who are ignorant of a work-life balance lifestyle to ask you how you do it, and I know surely that you would be selfless enough to guide them right.

Sub-Topic 2:

Three (3) Benefits Of Having A Work-Life Balanced Lifestyle

Truth be told, there are benefits and there are benefits. One set of benefits you as a fresh graduate should go all out to self-develop to achieve and enjoy in your career path is the set of benefits that comes from deliberately and faithfully practicing a work-life balanced lifestyle in your career journey in life. This is why it becomes necessary for me to include this sub-topic in this topic, so I can reveal to you three benefits you will enjoy when you consciously and consistently manage your work and life to always be in balance as you work and live. Let's get started!

1. A Work-Life Balanced Lifestyle Will Keep You In Charge Of Every Area Of Your Life.

As a fresh graduate, I want you to know that when you deliberately and faithfully practice a work-life balanced lifestyle from the start of your career journey and as you journey along your career path, you will be able to be in charge of every area of your life. True! Without any serious debate from you, you will agree with me that not being in charge of every area of your life could be very frustrating and disappointing as well, not only to you but by those who depend on you or look up to you. True! Therefore, to avoid this from happening to you in your career and life journey in the near future, you need to consciously and consistently commit to making sure your work and life are balanced always, and when you achieve this, it will help you stay on top of each and every area of your life. And I know this is what you truly want to see happen to you from the start of your career and along your career path. Am I right? I hear you say, yes, you are right. Thank you!

2. A Work-Life Balanced Lifestyle Will Keep You Fit And Relevant For A Long Time In Your Career And In Life.

As a fresh graduate, I want you to know that when you deliberately and faithfully practice a work-life balanced lifestyle from the start of your career journey and as you journey along your career path, you will be able to stay fit and relevant for a long time in your career and in life. True! Without any serious disagreement from you, you will agree with me that not being fit and relevant for a long time in your career and life could be very disheartening and disappointing as well, not only to you but to those who depend on you or look up to you. True! Therefore, to avoid this from happening to you in your career and life journey in the near future, you need to consciously and consistently commit to making sure your work and life are balanced always, and when you achieve this, it will help you stay fit and relevant for a long time in your career and in life. Again, I know this is what you truly want to see happen to you from the start of your career and along your career path. Am I right? I hear you say once more, yes, you are right. Thank you!

3. A Work-Life Balanced Lifestyle Will Keep You Involved In Other Important Areas Of Your Life.

As a fresh graduate, I want you to know that when you deliberately and faithfully practice a work-life balanced lifestyle from the start of your career journey and as you journey along your career path, you will be able to stay involved in other important areas of your life. True! Without any serious argument from you, you will agree with me that not being involved in other important areas of your life could be very disadvantageous and disappointing as well, not only to you but to those who depend on you or look up to you. True! Therefore, to avoid this happening to you in your career and life journey in the near future, you need to consciously and consistently commit to making sure your work and life are balanced always, and when you achieve this, it will help you stay involved in other important areas of your life. Once again, I know this is what you truly want to see happen to you from the start of your career and along your career path. Am I right? I hear you say it loud and clear; yes, you are right.

Sub-Topic 3

Three (3) Areas Of Your Life That You Must Always Keep Balanced With Your Work To Stay Healthy, Focused, And Productive Always

Having come this far with you on your need to be aware of what work-life balance is and the benefits you can derive from practicing a work-life balanced lifestyle from the start of your career and along your career journey, it becomes very important at this point for me to reveal to you three areas of your life that you must always keep balance with your work to stay healthy, focused, and productive. This is the reason this sub-topic becomes relevant to be included in this topic. So let's go!

1. Always Keep Your Work Life And Spiritual Life Balanced.

As a fresh graduate, I want you to know that to use a work-life balanced lifestyle to stay healthy, focused, and productive always in your career and in life, you need to consciously and consistently make sure your work is balanced with your spiritual life. This is to make sure the spiritual strength and power you need to stay healthy, focused, and productive is developed and available to you when you truly need it. This is because there will be times and seasons in your career and life when there will be unavoidable challenges and circumstances in your career path and life journey that you will surely need the spiritual strength and power you have built over time to overcome. This will be possible if you have not neglected and sacrificed your spiritual growth and development for only your career advancement. If you have not, you will stay healthy, focused, and productive in your career and in life. True! In achieving this, you should consciously and consistently make out time daily, weekly, monthly, and yearly to check, grow, and self-develop your spiritual life to be up to and above acceptable standards so that you will be spiritually fit and balanced for your life and career activities. If you do, you will be better for it. True! Some workers who are out of balance with their spiritual life because of their work-life commitment have to pay a price for allowing such an imbalance to happen to them. This must not be you, and that is why you must start right now by balancing your work life with your spiritual life always.

2. Always Keep Your Work Life And Mental And Moral Life Balanced.

As a fresh graduate, I want you to know that to use a work-life balanced lifestyle to stay healthy, focused, and productive always in your career and in life, you need to consciously and consistently make sure your work is balanced with your mental and moral life. This is to make sure the mental and moral strength and power you need to stay healthy, focused, and productive are developed and available to you when you truly need it. This is because there will be times and seasons in your career and life when there will be unavoidable challenges and circumstances in your career path and life journey when you will surely need mental and moral strength and power you have built over time to overcome. This will be possible if you have not neglected and sacrificed your mental and moral growth and development solely for your career advancement. If you have not, you will stay healthy, focused, and productive in your career and in life. True! In achieving this, you should consciously and consistently make out time daily, weekly, monthly, and yearly to check, grow, and self-develop your mental and moral life to be up to and above acceptable standards, so that you will be mentally and morally fit and balanced for your life and career activities. If you do, you will be better for it that you did. True! Many workers who are out of balance with their mental and moral lives because of their work-life commitment have paid greatly for allowing such an imbalance to happen to them. This must not be you, and that is why you must start right now by balancing your work life with your mental and moral life always.

3. Always Keep Your Work Life And Family And Friends' Lives Balanced.

As a fresh graduate, I want you to know that to use a work-life balanced lifestyle to stay healthy, focused, and productive always in your career and in life, you need to consciously and consistently make sure your work is balanced with your family and friends life. This is to make sure the family and friends' strength and power you need to stay healthy, focused, and productive are developed and available to you when you truly need it. This is because there will be times and seasons in your career and life when there will be unavoidable challenges and circumstances in your career path and life journey when you will surely need family and friends' strength and power you have built over time to overcome. This will be possible if you have not neglected and sacrificed your family and friends' relationships and welfare for your career advancement alone. If you have not, you will stay healthy, focused, and productive in your career and in life. True! In achieving this, you should consciously and consistently make out time daily, weekly, monthly, and yearly to check, relate with family members, and interact with friends reasonably and acceptably, so that you will be family and friends fit and balanced for your life and career activities. If you do, you will be better for it that you did. True! Many workers who are out of balance with their family and friends lives because of their work-life commitment have to pay a price for allowing such an imbalance to happen to them. This must not be you, and that is why you must start right now by balancing your work life with your family and friends' lives always.

Now, I have an assignment for you to do to get my message to you into you properly and perfectly. Take time to do them, and thank me later.

Assignment

- List every area of your life that you want to give your time and attention to.

- List the activities you usually and daily engage in that takes most of your time

- Compare your lists and see what you can do to balance both list. Do it urgently!

TOPIC 8: YOU AND YOUR JOB TRANSITION

Topic Objective

You will know what a job transition is and when to do it without fear or worry.

Sub-Topic 1

Three (3) Reasons Why You May Consider Job Transition As A Fresh Graduate

Another aspect I have discovered as a career coach, counselor, and mentor to many fresh graduates for over a decade is that many fresh graduates do not have the awareness at what point they should do job transition, that is, moving from one career path to another career path. This is because many fresh graduates do not know that they can encounter and experience along their career path someday a need to do a job transition from one career path to another career path for one reason or another. This has made many fresh graduates not consider job transition early enough. This has also made many fresh graduates unprepared to make this very important job transition move when necessary, or for some, it has made them make a wrong job transition decision and move that has caused them to regret their action much later. This must not be your own encounter and experience in your career journey. Therefore, my reason is to reveal to you three reasons why you may consider job transition as a fresh graduate. Let's begin!

1. When Your Career Choice Is Not In Line With Your Life Purpose

As a fresh graduate, I want you to know that you should consider the job transition of moving from one career path to another career path when your current career choice is not in line with your God-given life purpose. This is very important for you to do because the reason or reasons for making a career choice, pursuing a career path, or practicing a career should not just be for paying bills, acquiring material things, or achieving certain success in life. Making a career choice, pursuing a career path, or practicing a certain career should be more than just paying bills, acquiring material things, or achieving certain success in life, as it is for many people. True! You should go further than others to use your career choice, career pursuit, or career practice to attain fulfillment and satisfaction in life. In achieving this, you may need to consciously consider if you will need to do a job transition from your current career path, which has no connection to your God-given life purpose in life, to a career path you have discovered your God-given life purpose in life is connected to. This is an important consideration and decision to make as a fresh graduate because in no distant time in your career journey, when you have achieved your desired success and you can comfortably pay all your bills, you will come to realize that achieving just certain success in life and paying all your bills with your career choice, career pursuit, or career practice is not enough to give you the fulfillment and satisfaction in life that you have done what you existed on Earth for. This is because there will still be dissatisfaction and discontentment within you and a feeling not being fulfilled in life and in your career pursuit despite your career and life achievements. True! This I know you do not want to encounter and experience in the near future in your career journey. Therefore, my call for you to consider a job transition now if your current career path has no connection with your God-given life purpose or reason for existence on Earth you have discovered. Will you be bold enough to do this? I know you are!

2. When Your Career Choice Is Not In Line With Your Potential

As a fresh graduate, I want you to know that you should consider the job transition of moving from one career path to another when your current career choice is not in line with your God-given potential (talents or gifts) in life. This is very important you do because the reason or reasons for making a career choice, pursuing a career path, or practicing a career should not just be for paying bills, acquiring material things, or achieving certain successes in life. Making a career choice, pursuing a career path, or practicing a certain career should be more than just paying bills, acquiring material things, or achieving certain successes in life, as it is for many people. True! You should go further than others by using your career choice, career pursuit, or career practice to maximize your God-given potential in life. In achieving this, you may need to consciously consider if you will need to do a job transition from your current career path, which has no connection to your God-given potentials in life, to a career path you have discovered your God-given potentials in life are connected to. This is a very important consideration and decision to make as a fresh graduate because, in no distant time in your career journey, when you have achieved your desired success and you can comfortably pay all your bills, you will come to realize that achieving just certain successes in life and paying all your bills with your career choice, career pursuit, or career practice is not enough to give you the fulfillment and satisfaction in life that you have maximized your God-given potentials in life. This is because there will still be dissatisfaction and discontentment within you feeling unfulfilled in life and in your career pursuit despite your career and life achievements. True! I know you do not want to encounter or experience this in the near future in your career journey. Therefore, my call is for you to consider a job transition now if your current career path has no connection with your God-given potential (talents or gifts). Will you be courageous enough to do this? I know you are!

3. When Your Career Choice Is Not In Line With Your Personality

As a fresh graduate, I want you to know that you should consider the job transition of moving from one career path to another career path when your current career choice is not in line with your God-given personality in life. This is important for you to do because the reasons for making a career choice, pursuing a career path, or practicing a career should not just be for paying bills, acquiring material things, or achieving certain success in life. Making a career choice, pursuing a career path, or practicing a certain career should be more than just paying bills, acquiring material things, or achieving certain successes in life, as it is for many people. True! You should go further than others to use your career choice, career pursuit, or career practice to express your God-given personality in life. In achieving this, you may need to consciously consider if you will need to do a job transition from your current career path, which has no connection to your God-given personality in life, to a career path you have discovered your God-given personality in life is connected to. This is an important consideration and decision to make as a fresh graduate because in no distant time in your career journey, when you have achieved your desired success and you can comfortably pay all your bills, you will come to realize that achieving just certain successes and paying all your bills with your career choice, career pursue, or career practice is not enough to give you the fulfillment and satisfaction in life that you have expressed your God-given personality in life. This is because there will still be dissatisfaction and discontentment within you feeling unfulfilled in life and in your career pursuit despite your career and life achievements. True! I know you do not want to encounter or experience this in the near future in your career journey. Therefore, my call is for you to consider a job transition now if your current career path has no connection with the God-given personality you have discovered. Will you be courageous enough to do this? I know you are!

Sub-Topic 2

Three (3) Things To Consider Before Your Job Transition As A Fresh Graduate

Having encouraged you in sub-topic one to consider a job transition from your current career path to another career path if your current career choice is not connected to your God-given purpose, potential, and personality, I want to call on you that before you do your job transition, you should consider these three things I am about to reveal to you in this sub-topic because knowledge is power and powerful when applied rightly. Let's begin!

1. Consider If You Have The Right Required Information Before Your Job Transition.

As a fresh graduate, I want you to know that before you do your job transition, you should first and foremost consider if you have the right required information necessary for you to do your job transition. This is very important and necessary you do because a job transition done in ignorance or without the right required information could lead you to regret and sadness of heart in your new career path thereafter. Therefore, you should consciously and carefully consider if you have the right required information to do your job transition before you embark on your job transition to move from your current career path to another career path of your choice. This truly cannot be overemphasized. You should consciously and carefully search and research for relevant information about the new career path to make an informed decision. Now, until you are very sure and convinced that you have gotten the right required information necessary for you to do your job transition without doubts and worries, do not do it. If you follow this instruction, you will be better for it because you will save yourself from the immediate and future regrets if you do so. I know you will!

2. Consider If You Have The Right Required Qualifications Before Your Job Transition.

As a fresh graduate, I want you to know that before you do your job transition, you should next consider if you have the right required qualifications necessary for you to do your job transition. This is important and necessary you do because a job transition done without the right required qualifications could lead you to rejection and delay in your new career industry thereafter. Therefore, you should consciously and carefully consider if you have the right required qualifications to do your job transition before you embark on your job transition, moving from your current career path to another career path of your choice. This honestly cannot be overemphasized. In achieving this, you should consciously and painstakingly search and research for relevant qualification courses and certifications you need to have to qualify you for the new career path you are about to take. Until you are very sure and convinced that you have gotten the right required qualifications to do your job transition without doubts and worries, do not do it. If you do as I have just advised you, you will be better for it because you will save yourself from the immediate and future regrets if you do so. I know you will!

3. Consider If You Have The Right Required Finance And Support Before Your Job Transition.

As a fresh graduate, I want you to know that before you do your job transition, you should consider if you have the right required finance and support necessary for you to do your job transition. This is important and quite necessary for you to do because a job transition done without the right required finance and support could lead to an unfinished transition in your new career move thereafter. Therefore, you should consciously and carefully consider if you have the right required finance and support to do your job transition before you embark on your job transition to move from your current career path to another career path of your choice. This too cannot be overemphasized. In achieving this, you should consciously and patiently make and save the required money or seek financial support (or other relevant supports) you need to qualify you for the new career path you are about to take. Now, until you are very sure and convinced that you have gotten the right required finance and support to do your job transition without doubts and worries, do not do it. If you do as I have just counseled you, you will be better for it because you will save yourself from the immediate and future regrets if you do so. I know.

Sub-Topic 3

Three (3) Ways Not To Do A Job Transition As A Fresh Graduate

While it is good to have knowledge about something, it is better and even best to know how to do it right or how not to do it wrong. This is the reason I included this sub-topic in this topic to help you know ways you should not do your job transition. Therefore, in this sub-topic, I will be revealing to you three ways you should not do your job transition as a fresh graduate. Let's roll!

1. Never Do A Job Transition When You Are Not Very Sure Of Your New Career Path.

As a fresh graduate, I want you to know that you should not do your job transition when you are not very sure if your new career path is for you or not. This is because your uncertainty and doubt may cause you to make a wrong career choice or follow a wrong career path in life. True! Therefore, you should not do your job transition when you are not certain or very sure of your new career choice or career path you want to take. This is important for you to know and take to heart when considering your job transition as a fresh graduate. In achieving this, you should always take time to think thoroughly to know if your new career choice or career path you are about to follow is right for you or not. That is, if your new career choice or career path you are about to take aligns with your God-given purpose, potential, and personality in life or not. Again, this is important for you to do, and if you do, you will not regret your job transition decision now or in the near future. I know this is what you want happen to you because now you know better, and like I stated before, knowledge is power, but applied knowledge is powerful. As needed, you will use this knowledge to your advantage.

2. Never Do A Job Transition When You Are Only Wanting To Do So Because Of Pressure From Family And Friends.

As a fresh graduate, I want you to know that you should not do your job transition when you are only wanting to do so because of pressure from family and friends. This is because not being able to take an unforced decision on your job transition may cause you to make the wrong career choice or follow the wrong career path in life. True! Therefore, you should not do your job transition when you are under pressure to do so without giving liberty to make your own new career choice or take the career path you want to take. This is important for you to know and take to heart when considering your job transition as a fresh graduate. In achieving this, you should learn to always take the final decision on your job transition after taking suggestions from family and friends. This means that you should make sure that your new career choice or career path you are about to take aligns with your God-given purpose, potential, and personality in life, no matter the pressure from family and friends. This is very important for you to do, and if you do, you will not have a reason to regret your job transition decision now or in the near future. I know this is what you want to happen to you because now you know better, and like I stated before, knowledge is power, but applied knowledge is powerful. As needed, you will use this knowledge to your advantage.

3. Never Do A Job Transition When You Have Not Discovered Your Life Purpose, Potential, And Personality.

As a fresh graduate, I want you to know that you should not do your job transition when you have not discovered your life purpose, potential, and personality. This is because for you to have your career choice or career practice not only to pay bills, get you material possessions, and achieve certain success for you in life, but also to attain fulfillment and satisfaction for you in life, your job transition to a new career choice or career path should align with your God-given purpose, potential, and personality. True! If these are not known, you may make the wrong career choice or follow the wrong career path in life. True! Therefore, you should not do your job transition when you are not certain or very sure of your God-given purpose, potential, and personality in life that are supposed to guide you in your job transition to a new career choice or career path you should take. This is important for you to know and take to heart when considering your job transition as a fresh graduate. In achieving this, you should first and foremost prayerfully seek God for knowledge of your purpose, potential, and personality, and watchfully observe yourself from your past to now to see what and what has gotten your attention (cause you pain or given joy passionately), and you can do anything for free, whether you are paid for it or not, to address those issues in other people's lives. That might just be your God-given purpose that you need to pay attention to right now, which aligns with your career choice. Then, what potentials (talents or gifts) and personalities you have observed you have or other people have consistently commended you for over the years. Again, that may just be your God-given potential and personality you need to now pay close attention to right now and align your career choice with. This is very important for you to do, and if you do, you will not have a need to regret your job transition decision now or in the near future. I know this is what you want to happen to you because now you know better, and like I stated before, knowledge is power, but applied knowledge is powerful. I know you will apply this knowledge when and where necessary to your benefit and profit.

My assignment is to practically instill this topic's message in you. Do it, and get better at it.

Assignment

- Based on your understanding of job transition, do a quick and thorough check within the next 21 days if you need to do job transition as a fresh graduate.

TOPIC 9: YOU AND YOUR SELF-EMPLOYMENT

Topic Objective:

You Will Be Able To See And Take Advantage Of The Advantages Of Self-Employment To Advance Yourself.

Sub-Topic 1:

Three (3) Reasons Why You Should Consider Self-Employment As A Fresh Graduate

The pride and honor of being a graduate from a higher institution (university or college) has made many fresh graduates not consider self-employment as an alternative option to explore, or route they could go through to achieve success and satisfaction in life. True! I discovered over the years that the mindset of many fresh graduates after school is to get a paid job, nothing more, nothing less. This is why I included this topic in this book and this sub-topic in this topic. Therefore, in this sub-topic, I will be revealing to you three reasons why you should consider self-employment as a fresh graduate. Are you ready? Let's go!

1. You Should Consider Self-Employment Because It Might Just Be Right For You.

As a fresh graduate, I want you to know that you should consider self-employment as an alternative option to paid employment that you could explore or route you could go through to achieve success and satisfaction in life. This is because self-employment could be right for you as a fresh graduate. True! This becomes very important for you to take into consideration because we are all not designed and destined by God to do paid jobs or be in paid employment in life after schooling or with our entire lifetime on Earth. Therefore, it is wise and smart for you to consciously consider self-employment as an alternative option or route you can use to achieve success and satisfaction in life to see if it is right for you or not. In achieving this, you should consciously and thoughtfully take out reasonable time to do self-check to see if you are designed and destined by God to explore and employ the self-employment option or route to achieve success and satisfaction in life from the start of your career journey and not paid employment. This is important for you to know and do now when you are about to start your career journey in life. If you do, you might just be on your way of establishing a global idea that will shock the world and benefit humanity for a long time. True! This is the way many global organizations that many fresh graduates desire to be part of started. Therefore, if you consider self-employment as an alternative option or route to achieve success and satisfaction in life, as I am encouraging you to do, you might just be on your way to setting up a global brand that will employ lots of other fresh graduates in the near future. True! Give it a try.

2. You Should Consider Self-Employment Because It Will Pay Your Bills While You Wait To Be Employed In A Paid Job.

As a fresh graduate, I want you to know that you should consider self-employment as an alternative option to paid employment. You could explore or route you could use alternatively to pay your bills and meet your other financial needs for the main time while you wait for a paid employment job. This is because there are self-employment options available that you could use temporarily to pay your bills and to take care of your other financial needs as a fresh graduate waiting to be employed in a paid job. True! This becomes very necessary for you to take into consideration because, as a fresh graduate from school into the labor market, you may need to pay some bills and meet other of your financial needs before you are engaged or employed by your desired paid employment organization. Therefore, it is wise and smart for you to consider self-employment as an alternative option or route you can use to temporarily pay your bills and meet your other financial needs before you are hired by a paid employment organization. In achieving this, you should consciously and humbly consider a self-employment option or route for paying your bills and meeting other of your financial needs by going all out to search and see which self-employment options or routes fit your financial needs and exploring them immediately because you have bills to pay and financial needs to meet while you wait for your desired paid employment option. True! This is important for you to know and do now when you are about to start your career journey in life. If you do, you might not just be using self-employment to pay your bills or meet your financial needs; you might just be on your way of discovering a self-employment idea that you might explore to become one of the world's leading self-employed entrepreneurs of our times. True! Again, this is the way many global organizations that many fresh graduates desire to be part of started. Therefore, if you consider self-employment as an alternative option or route to pay your bills and meet your financial needs, as I am encouraging you to do, you might not just relieve yourself from financial burdens; you might just be on your way to setting up a global brand that will employ lots of other fresh graduates in the near future. True! Give it a try.

3. You Should Consider Self-Employment Because Age Is Still On Your Side To Build Something Great For Yourself And Your Family.

As a fresh graduate, I want you to know that you should consider self-employment as an alternative option to paid employment you could explore or route you could go through because age is still on your side to build something great for yourself and your family. This is because, as a fresh graduate who still has an age advantage, self-employment could be right for you to build something amazing for yourself and your family rather than waiting for paid employment. True! This becomes very important for you to take into consideration because if self-employment is designed and destined for you by God to use to achieve financial freedom, greatness, and satisfaction in life, realizing and starting now that you are young is a far better option than realizing and starting later in life. This is also because building something great might take some reasonable time. Therefore, it is wise and smart for you to consciously consider self-employment as an alternative option or route you can use to build something amazing and great for yourself and your family when you are still a fresh graduate who is still young and vibrant in life. In achieving this, you should consciously and thoughtfully take out reasonable time to do self-check to see if you are designed and destined by God to explore and employ the self-employment option or route to build something great for yourself and your family from the start of your career journey and not paid employment. This is important for you to know and do now when you are about to start your career journey in life and age is still in your side and favor. If you do, you might just be on your way of establishing a global organization that will shock the world and benefit not just yourself and your family but humanity for a long time. True! Again, as I have said before, this is the way many global organizations that many fresh graduates desire to be part of started. Therefore, if you consider self-employment as an alternative option or route to build something great for yourself and your family, as I am encouraging you to do, you might just be on your way to setting up a global name that will employ lots of other fresh graduates in the near future. True! Give it a try.

Sub-Topic 2:

Three (3) Benefits of Becoming Self-Employed As A Fresh Graduate

To encourage you further to consider self-employment as an alternative option for you to explore or route to go through to achieve success and satisfaction in life as a fresh graduate, I want to reveal to you three benefits of becoming a self-employed as a fresh graduate. This becomes necessary because over the years I have not only heard but seen many fresh graduates who ignorantly detest the word self-employment and do not want to do anything with it as an alternative option for them to paid employ. Again, this is sad! So, let's go!

1. Self-Employment Offers You The Opportunity To Discover Your Life Purpose.

As a fresh graduate, I want you to know that if you consider self-employment as an alternative option or route to go through, self-employment offers you the opportunity to discover your God-given purpose in life. This means that self-employment has the ability to reveal areas of you that you had no knowledge about yourself before. This is very true! Therefore, I encourage you to do a thorough self-check and research to see if self-employment is right for you or not. In achieving this, you need now to consciously consider and painstakingly make up reasonable time to explore and employ self-employment as a means to discover your God-given purpose in life. That is, as a way of discovering your real reason for existence in this world. If you do, you would have succeeded in coming to the awareness of who you truly are, and this is a very important knowledge of yourself that you could use as a guide to achieve not only success in life but also satisfaction in life. True! I know that achieving satisfaction in life matters to you because it should. Give self-employment a try now!

2. Self-Employment Offers You The Opportunity To Develop Your Potential.

As a fresh graduate, I want you to know that if you consider self-employment as an alternative option or route to go through, self-employment offers you the opportunity to develop your God-given potential in life. This means that self-employment has the capability to grow and develop areas of you that you had no knowledge about before. This is very true! Therefore, I encourage you to do a thorough self-check and research to see if self-employment is right for you or not. In achieving this, you need now to consciously consider and painstakingly make up reasonable time to explore and employ self-employment as a means to develop your God-given potentials in life. That is, as a way of developing your real talents and gifts you have in this world. If you do, you would have succeeded in coming to the knowledge of your true capacity and competence of who you truly are, and this is a very important knowledge of yourself that you could use as a guide to achieve not only success in life but also satisfaction in life. True! I know that achieving satisfaction in life matters to you because it should. Give self-employment a chance today!

- Self-Employment Offers You The Opportunity To Deliver Your Purpose, Potential, And Personality To The World.

As a fresh graduate, I want you to know that if you consider self-employment as an alternative option or route to go through, self-employment offers you the opportunity to deliver your God-given purpose, potential, and personality in life to the world. This means that self-employment has the avenue to allow areas of you that you had no knowledge about previously to express themselves to others. This is very true! Therefore, I encourage you to do a thorough self-check and research to see if self-employment is right for you or not. In achieving this, you need now to consciously consider and painstakingly make up reasonable time to explore and employ self-employment as a means to deliver your God-given purpose, potential, and personality in life to the world. That is, as a way of delivering your real reason for existence, real talents and gifts, and real charisma you have in this world to others. If you do, you would have succeeded in fully manifesting and maximizing yourself to the world and also achieve not only success in life but also satisfaction in life. True! I know you value success and happiness because you should. Give self-employment a try today!

Sub-Topic 3:

Three (3) Ways To Transit Into Self-Employment As A Fresh Graduate

While I know you are now convinced that self-employment could be an alternative option you can explore or route you could go as a fresh graduate, I want you to know that there are ways to transit into self-employment. Therefore, in this lesson I will be revealing to you three ways you should transit after you decide to consider a self-employment option or route in your career journey to success and satisfaction in life. Let's roll!

1. By Exploring Your Own Idea Or Other Ideas Discovered

As a fresh graduate, I want you to know that one way you can transit into self-employment is by considering exploring your own ideas or other ideas discovered, including ideas within your workplace if you are already employed. True! It will interest you to know that over the years, you have consciously or unconsciously generated many ideas for self-employment that you never paid attention to. That might just be a divine call within you to consider self-employment. True! For some of these ideas, you may have written them down, and for some you could not even remember any longer. Whichever way, take those ideas you have written down before and add those you could remember because it is time to pay attention to them all to see which one you could use to start your self-employment journey in life. This becomes important for you to do. As I have said several times, self-employment could just be the right employment for you to use to achieve success and satisfaction in life like any other paid employment. True! In achieving this, it is time for you to consciously consider self-employment as an alternative option or route to go and painstakingly go into your archives to bring out those ideas you have written down over the years because the time to see if you could actually begin one or two of those ideas has finally come. Furthermore, if you cannot remember any idea coming to mind, you might need to be sensitive and observant to see if you can get an idea in other places, including your workplace if you are currently employed. You could take a look at what you are doing in your workplace or someone else is doing to see if you can get an outstanding hidden idea from it and see if you can explore it to enter the self-employment route in life. If you do, you might just be on your way to delivering outstanding goods or services to the world, which you could use to achieve success and satisfaction in life. True!

2. By Humbly Learning A Trade Or Engaging In A Vocational Internship Program

As a fresh graduate, I want you to know that another way you can transit into self-employment is by considering humbling yourself as a fresh graduate to learn a trade you have interest in or enrolling in a vocational internship program for some time to learn some skills. True! It will interest you to know that over the years, you may have consciously or unconsciously within you been nursing a trade or set of skills you would have loved to develop or learn that you never gave attention to. That might just be a divine call within you to consider self-employment. True! This is the time to once again consider those thoughts of learning a trade or developing a skill you have nursed these past years and give attention to them now. This is because the time for you to consider learning a trade or a skill as a fresh graduate who wants to start a career journey of a lifetime is now, so that you can start your own self-employment journey in life. This becomes very important for you to do, as I have said before, and I will love to say it here again because self-employment could just be the right employment for you to use to achieve success and satisfaction in life like any other paid employment. True! In achieving this, it is time for you to consciously consider self-employment as an alternative option or route to go and humbly go all out to search and research trades you could learn or skills you could develop that you have been nursing within you over the years and see thereafter if you can explore it to enter the self-employment route in life. If you do, you might just be on your way to delivering outstanding goods or services to the world, which you could use to achieve success and satisfaction in life. True!

3. By Understudying Another Self-Employed Person

As a fresh graduate, I want you to know that one more way you can transit into self-employment is by considering understudying another self-employed person or entrepreneur to understand for some time what it takes to start and run such person's area of business or service. True! It will interest you to know that over the years, you have consciously or unconsciously within you a hidden desire to understand what someone you admired over the years is doing, and because of what others would say, you have not paid real attention to it. That might just be a divine call within you to consider self-employment. True! This is the time to once again consider taking a step further by actually going to discuss this out with such a person or entrepreneur so that you can start your understudy program with him or her. This is because the time to consider starting your understudying program is now as a fresh graduate who wants to start a career journey of a lifetime so that you can start your own self-employment journey in life. This becomes very important for you to do because self-employment could just be the right employment for you to use to achieve success and satisfaction in life like any other paid employment. True! In achieving this, it is time for you to consciously consider self-employment as an alternative option or route to go and take a bold step toward understudying under a self-employed person or entrepreneur you have been admiring over the years and see thereafter if you can explore it to enter the self-employment route in life. If you do, you might just be on your way to delivering outstanding goods or services to the world, which you could use to achieve success and satisfaction in life. True!

Now, I have an assignment for you to do, so you can get the message in this topic internalized in you. Please, do it.

Assignment

- Based on your current understanding of self-employment, do a quick and thorough check within the next 14 days if you need to get into the self-employment route.

TOPIC 10: YOU AND YOUR DIVINE DESTINY WORK

Topic Objective

You Will Be Able To Know The Career Path For Yourself To Success, Satisfaction, And Significance In Life.

Sub-Topic 1:

Three (3) Things You Need To Urgently Know About Your Divine Destiny Work As A Fresh Graduate

As I conclude this book with this topic, I want to state here that my encounter and experience with many fresh graduates reveal to me that many fresh graduates are ignorant or have no knowledge about their divine destiny work in life. Therefore, many fresh graduates have gone ahead to choose and practice professions that have nothing to do with their God-given purpose, potential, and personality in life. Therefore, having come this far with me in this book, it will be an injustice to you if I do not let you know about Divine Destiny Work. So in this lesson, I will be revealing to you three things you need to urgently know about your Divine Destiny Work so that you are no longer among those fresh graduates who are unaware of this. Let's get started!

1. Your Divine Destiny Work Is Your Prophetic Life Purpose Profession; You Should Have Discovered And Made Your Career Path In Life.

As a fresh graduate, I want you to urgently know that there is a prophetic life-purpose profession for you on Earth, which I call your Divine Destiny Work. This is a profession you should have discovered and made your career choice and career path in life before you start schooling and after you have discovered your prophetic life purpose on Earth or God-given purpose in life. This is a profession you should have chosen out of a place of prayer and inspiration, then studied in school and now want to practice in life as a fresh graduate. It is a profession you select among other professions, whether you love it or not. It is a profession you accept to run with in life, whether it pays your bills or not. It is a profession you practice not only to achieve success and greatness in life but also to achieve true satisfaction and significance in life. Therefore, it is a profession amongst other professions that connects you to your real reason for existence on earth. In achieving this, you might need now to consciously consider discovering your God-given purpose in life and thoughtfully consider doing a job transition to correct this error if your current profession has nothing to do with your God-given purpose in life. True! If you courageously and sacrificially do, you will have no regret in the near future taking this decision because you would not only have achieved success and greatness in life then, but you would also have achieved satisfaction and significance in life. True! I know this is what you are really craving in life. Yes, I know! So give it a try now!

2. Your Divine Destiny Work Is Designed To Work In Unity With Your Potential.

As a fresh graduate, I want you to urgently know that your Divine Destiny Work (prophetic life purpose profession) on Earth was designed by God to work in unity with God-given potentials (talents and gifts) in life. This is a profession you first and foremost should have discovered had a connection with your God-given potentials in life before you made it your career choice and career path in life and then before you started schooling. This is a profession you should have chosen out of a place of prayer and inspiration, then studied in school and now want to practice in life as a fresh graduate because you have also found out that it works perfectly with your God-given gifts and talents in life. It is a profession you select among other professions not because you love it or not, but because it fits perfectly with your God-given potential, which you have discovered you have. It is a profession you accept to run with in life not because it pays your bills or not, but because it is in alignment with your God-given talents and gifts. It is a profession you practice not only to achieve success, greatness, satisfaction, and significance in life but also to maximize your God-given potential. True! Therefore, it is a profession amongst other professions that connects you to your real gifts and talents on earth. In achieving this, you might need now to consciously consider discovering your God-given potentials in life and thoughtfully consider doing a job transition to correct this error if your current profession has nothing to do with your God-given talents and gifts in life. True! If you boldly and sacrificially do, you will have no regret in the near future taking this decision because you would not only have achieved success, greatness, satisfaction, and significance in life, but you would also have made use of your God-given potentials to the maximum. True! Again, I know this is what you really desire happened to you in life. Yes, I know this, too! So, give it a try!

3. Your Divine Destiny Work Is Designed To Work In Harmony With Your Personality.

As a fresh graduate, I want you to know that your Divine Destiny Work (prophetic life purpose profession) on Earth was designed by God to work in harmony with God-given personality (character and charisma) in life. This is a profession you should have discovered had a link with your God-given personality in life before you made it your career choice and career path in life and then before you started schooling. This is a profession you should have chosen out of a place of prayer and inspiration, then studied in school and now want to practice in life as a fresh graduate because you have also found out that it works perfectly with your God-given character and charisma in life. It is a profession you select among other professions not because you love it or not, but because it fits squarely with your God-given personality you have discovered. It is a profession you accept to run with in life not because it pays your bills or not, but because it is in alignment harmoniously with your God-given personality. It is a profession you practice not only to achieve success, greatness, satisfaction, and significance in life but also to express your God-given character and charisma. True! Therefore, it is a profession amongst other professions that connects you to your real personality on earth. In achieving this, you might need now to consciously consider discovering your God-given personality in life and thoughtfully consider doing a job transition to correct this error if your current profession has nothing to do with your God-given personality (character and charisma) in life. True! If you confidently and sacrificially do, you will have no regret in the near future taking this decision because you would not only have achieved success, greatness, satisfaction, and significance in life, but you would also have expressed your God-given personality to the fullest. True! I know this is what you are really aiming at in your career pursuit in life. Yes, I know this! So give it a try now! Thank you for listening.

Sub-Topic 2

Three (3) Advantages Of Practicing Your Divine Destiny Work As A Fresh Graduate

Like I have said once in the cause of this book, there are advantages and there are advantages. I discovered that many fresh graduates do not know that one of their considerations and actions in life that will give them unusual and uncommon advantages in life and in their career is the consideration and action of deciding to take up and practice their God-given Divine Destiny Work (prophetic life purpose profession) that lines up with their God-given purpose, potential, and personality in life. True! Therefore, in this sub-topic, I will reveal to you three advantages of practicing your Divine Destiny Work (life purpose profession) in life. Let's go!

1. Practicing Your Prophetic Life Purpose Profession Will Make You Outstanding And Extraordinary In Your Career Industry

As a fresh graduate, I want you to know that when you practice your God-given Divine Destiny Work (prophetic life purpose profession) on Earth, it will make you outstanding and extraordinary in your career industry. True! This is because you will be divinely manifesting and expressing your true reason of existence (life purpose), true gifts and talents (potentials), and true character and charisma (personality) on Earth. This is amazing! This is the secret of many of the seeming outstanding and extraordinary persons you see in your career industry or other career industries. That is, those in your career industry or other career industries you so admire and honor in your career industry. True! Therefore, I once again encourage you to thoughtfully consider practicing your Divine Destiny Work (prophetic life purpose profession) in life no matter what and against all odds instead of any other profession that has no link with your God-given purpose, potential, and personality in life. In achieving this, you should consciously and painstakingly consider seeking to discover your God-given purpose, potential, and personality in life if you have not already done so. Then carefully and objectively check if your current profession or career path aligns with them. If your current profession is not in agreement with your God-given purpose, potential, and personality in life, then urgently consider doing a job transition to a profession that fits perfectly with your God-given purpose, potential, and personality in life. If you courageously and sacrificially do so, you will be better for it, knowing that you will not just achieve success and greatness in life with your career path but also satisfaction and significance in life. More importantly, you would have manifested and expressed your real self to the world. And this is wonderful and great!

2. Practicing Your Prophetic Life Purpose Profession Will Make You Supernatural And A Role Model In Your Career Industry.

As a fresh graduate, I want you to know that when you practice your God-given Divine Destiny Work (prophetic life purpose profession) on Earth, it will make you supernatural and a role model in your career industry. True! This is because you will both be naturally and supernaturally manifesting and expressing your true reason of existence (life purpose), true gifts and talents (potentials), and true character and charisma (personality) on Earth. This is once again amazing! As I earlier said, this is the secret of many of the seemingly high-flying people you see in your career industry or other career industries. That is, those in your career industry or other career industries you so admire and honor in your career industry. True! Therefore, I encourage you to deeply consider practicing your Divine Destiny Work (prophetic life purpose profession) in life no matter what and against all odds instead of any other profession that has no real connection with your God-given purpose, potential, and personality in life. In achieving this, you should consciously and painstakingly consider seeking to discover your God-given purpose, potential, and personality in life if you have not already done so. Then carefully and objectively check if your current profession or career path aligns with them. If your current profession is not in alignment with your God-given purpose, potentials, and personality in life, then urgently consider doing a job transition to a profession that fits perfectly with your God-given purpose, potentials, and personality in life. If you boldly and sacrificially do so, you will be better for it, knowing that you will not just achieve success and greatness in life with your career journey but also satisfaction and significance in life. More importantly, you would have manifested and expressed your real self to the world's amazement. And this is once again good and great!

3. Practicing Your Prophetic Life Purpose Profession Will Make You Feel Peaceful And Fulfilled In Your Career Path.

.As a fresh graduate, I want you to know that when you practice your God-given Divine Destiny Work (prophetic life purpose profession) on Earth, it will make you feel peaceful and fulfilled in your career path. True! This is because you are manifesting and expressing your true reason of existence (life purpose), true gifts and talents (potentials), and true character and charisma (personality) on Earth that are in harmony with your Creator's desire for you on Earth. True! This is once again amazing and also wonderful! Again, this is the secret of many of the seemingly highly rated persons you see in your career industry or other career industries. That is, those in your career industry or other career industries you so admire and honor. True! Therefore, I encourage you to passionately consider practicing your Divine Destiny Work (prophetic life purpose profession) in life no matter what and against all odds instead of any other profession that has no real connection with your God-given purpose, potential, and personality in life. In achieving this, you should consciously and painstakingly consider seeking to discover your God-given purpose, potential, and personality in life if you have not already done so. Then carefully and objectively check if your current profession or career path aligns with them. If your current profession is not in alignment with your God-given purpose, potentials, and personality in life, then consider urgently doing a job transition to a profession that fits squarely with your God-given purpose, potentials, and personality in life. If you boldly and sacrificially do, you will be better for it knowing that you will not just achieve success and greatness in life with your career journey, but also satisfaction and significance in life. More importantly, you would have manifested and expressed your real self to the amazement of the world. And this is once again, good and great! Thank you for listening.

Sub-Topic 3

Three (3) Disadvantages Of Not Practicing Your Divine Destiny Work As A Fresh Graduate

As I conclude this topic and this book, I am glad that you have come to know what Divine Destiny Work is and the advantages of practicing your prophetic life-purpose profession. In this lesson, I want to go further to reveal to you three disadvantages you have if you do not consider and actually practice your Divine Destiny work as a fresh graduate. So let's roll!

1. Not Practicing Your Prophetic Life Purpose Profession Could Lead You Into A Struggling Mode In Life And In Your Career.

As a fresh graduate, I want you to know that not consciously considering and actually practicing your divine destiny work (prophetic life purpose profession) in life could lead you into a struggling mode in life. This is because you will be working against your true self as designed and destined by God, your Creator. Furthermore, this is because you will be working in complete misalignment to your God-given purpose, potential, and personality in life. That is, not working in agreement with your true reason for existence, true talents and gifts, and true character and charisma in life. This is sad! Therefore, I am calling your attention to this now and encouraging you to urgently check it out and correct this costly mistake if the current profession you have studied in school and are about to go all out to practice in the world has no real connection to your God-given purpose, potential, and personality in life. This is very important and urgent for you to consider now and to do something about it. In achieving this, you need to start now to seek to discover your

God-given purpose, potential, and personality in life and then consider a job transition if your current career path does not align with your discoveries of yourself. True! If you do this as I have counseled you, the sky will not be your ending point but a starting point. True! Again, you will not just achieve success in life in the near future, but satisfaction in it as well.

2. Not Practicing Your Prophetic Life Purpose Profession Could Lead You Into Survival Mode In Life And In Your Career.

As a fresh graduate, I want you to know that not consciously considering and actually practicing your divine destiny work (prophetic life purpose profession) in life could lead you into survival mode in life. This is because you will be working against your true self as designed and destined by God, your Creator. Furthermore, this is because you will be working in complete disagreement with your God-given purpose, potential, and personality in life. That is, working not in agreement with your true reason for existence, true talents and gifts, and true character and charisma in life. This is ridiculous! Therefore, I am calling your attention to this now and encouraging you to urgently check it out and correct this costly mistake if the current profession you have studied in school and are about to go all out to practice in the world has no real connection to your God-given purpose, potential, and personality in life. This is very important and urgent for you to consider now and to do something about it. In achieving this, you need to start now to seek to discover your God-given purpose, potential, and personality in life and then consider a job transition if your current career path does not align with your discoveries of yourself. True! If you do this as I have counseled you, again, the sky will not be your ending point but a starting point. True! You will not just achieve greatness in life in the near future, but fulfillment in it as well.

3. Not Practicing Your Prophetic Life Purpose Profession Could Lead You Into Minimized And Unfulfilled Use Of Your Potential And Personality In Life.

As a fresh graduate, I want you to know that not consciously considering and actually practicing your Divine Destiny work (prophetic life purpose profession) in life could lead you into minimized and unfulfilled use of your potentials and personality in life. Because you won't manifest your true self as God, your Creator, intended. Furthermore, this is because you will not be working in the direction of fulfilling your God-given purpose, maximizing your God-given potential, and expressing your God-given personality in life. That is, working not to meet up with your true reason for existence, true talents and gifts, and true character and charisma in life. This is not right! Therefore, I am calling your attention to this now and encouraging you to urgently check it out and correct this costly mistake if the current profession you have studied in school and are about to go all out to practice in the world has no real motivation and inspiration in you to meet up to your God-given purpose, potential, and personality in life. This is very important and urgent for you to consider now and to do something about it. In achieving this, you need to start now to seek to discover your God-given purpose, potential, and personality in life and then consider a job transition if your current career path does not stir up to catch up with your discoveries of yourself. True! If you do this as I have counseled you, again, the sky will not be your ending point but a starting point. True! You will not just achieve success and greatness in life in the near future, but satisfaction and fulfillment in life as well.

Now, I have an assignment for you to do to help you internalize the information in this sub-topic. Take out time to do it. Thank you for reading this book. Much love from me to you!

Assignment

- Make conscious and consistent effort to discover your divine destiny work (prophetic life purpose profession) in the next 100 days and consider following that path.

- Make conscious and consistent effort to discover your potential in the next 60 days and consider developing and putting them to use.

- Make a conscious and consistent effort to discover your personality in the next 30 days and consider developing and putting it to use.

SECTION B: GETTING YOU EXPOSED PRACTICALLY AS A FRESH GRADUATE

YOU AND YOUR PRACTICAL PREPARATION

It gives me so much joy to have worked on these ten topics with you. I know that a lot of timely, uncommon, and unusual information has been revealed and passed down to you. These are pieces of information you can use to have a right start to success and significance in life and career as a fresh graduate. Information you need not only to achieve success but also satisfaction and significance in life. Because you have been faithful to go through these 10 topics, I want to be involved not only in your theoretical preparation but also in your practical preparation.

To assist you in your life and career practical preparation, I will be admitting you into my social media community, 'Fresh Graduates' Life and Career Coaching for Success and Significance in Life Community,' where you can ask questions in any area of need in your life and career for 30 days from the day I added you to my community.

In order to receive this assistance from me, I will need you to send the following details to freshgraduatescoach@gmail.com:

Proof of your genuine purchase of the original copy of Fresh Graduates Right Start to Success and Significance

- Full name

- **WhatsApp number**

- **Email address**

See you then, love you!

www.ingramcontent.com/pod-product-compliance
Lightning Source LLC
Chambersburg PA
CBHW070543160726
48003CB00005B/1861